MARY
QUEEN OF SCOTS

GEDDES & GROSSET

This edition published 2000 by Geddes & Grosset, an imprint
of Children's Leisure Products Limited

© 2000 Children's Leisure Products Limited, David Dale
House, New Lanark ML11 9DJ, Scotland

ISBN 1 85534 920 5

Printed and bound in India

CONTENTS

CHAPTER I

THE EARLY REIGN

Born in Linlithgow in 1542 to Mary of Guise, while her father, James V of Scotland, was on his deathbed, in her early years Mary Stuart, Queen of Scots, ruled under successive regencies and was courted by contending factions: on the one hand the bigotry of the Catholic Church and on the other the intolerance and ambition of Henry VIII, who sought to unite England and Scotland by persuading her to marry his son, Edward, Prince of Wales. At the age of six, a beautiful, winsome child with deep hazel eyes and auburn hair, she was placed under the care of the King of France to be educated, and was engaged to the Dauphin, Francis, in order to thwart Henry's plans, which were later frustrated anyway by the early death of King Edward VI. Her early education under Cardinal Beaton left her a staunch Catholic, out of tune with the growing spirit of Reformism among the majority of her subjects back in Scotland.

Mary married Francis in 1558, at the age of sixteen. Not long afterwards, her namesake, Mary of England, died and Elizabeth, Mary's sister, succeeded to the throne. This event was to have a marked effect on the later history and life of the unfortunate Queen of Scots, and any consideration of the subsequent relationship between the two queens and Elizabeth's cruel treatment of Mary must take into account the fact that Mary had deeply offended her.

In June 1536, on the execution of Anne Boleyn, the English Parliament had declared both the daughters of Henry VIII to be illegitimate and had vested the succession in the children of Lady Jane Seymour, whom the king then married. Despite this and the attempt to secure a Protestant succession on the death of Edward VI in the person of Lady Jane Grey, the English people would have none of it. Mary Tudor succeeded her brother without any formal protest from the Queen of Scots about her claims to the English throne as the next heir of Henry VIII. However, on the death of Mary of England, the Queen of Scots unwisely adopted a different policy, and on 6 July 1559 made a public assertion of her claims in Paris, when she made a procession in a carriage emblazoned with the arms of both England and Scotland with heralds proclaiming her 'Queen of England'.

The Protestant Queen Elizabeth probably never forgave this insult to her mother and to herself, which contrasted with Mary's previous silent acceptance of the succession of the Catholic daughter of Catherine of Aragon as the legitimate heir to the English throne. It may almost be said that by conducting that procession and proclamation, Mary signed her own death warrant.

In the celebrations that followed, the King of France died in an accident. Mary's husband succeeded as Francis II, but died suddenly on 5 December the following year. The Queen Mother of Scotland, Mary of Guise, regent of Scotland in her daughter's absence, also died in June 1560.

During these few years the character and religious views of the Scottish people underwent a startling transformation. The activities of John Knox and his Congregational adherents spread the spirit of Reformation throughout the kingdom, and after the death of her husband so soon after that of her mother, at the age of nineteen Mary returned to Scotland in August 1561 to find a vastly different country, politically and religiously, from the one she had left twelve years earlier.

At the time of her return, young as she was, she was loving, tolerant and tactful, and her answers to the English ambassadors who tried to persuade her to ratify the Treaty of Edinburgh, abrogating her claim to the throne of England, show a remarkable degree of caution and diplomacy. She was very beautiful, and her Privy Council were desperate for her to remarry. She was courted by some of the greatest kings and princes of Europe, the Kings of Sweden and Denmark, the Archduke of Austria and the Prince of Spain all making formal proposals.

Her arrival in Scotland was greeted with joy, but the religious intolerance of the Congregationalists very soon caused serious trouble. Knox immediately led a demonstration against the celebration of mass in her private chapel at Holyrood, and Lord Lindsay of the Byres even threatened to murder her priests. Although Mary issued a proclamation that she would defend and maintain the Protestant religion in Scotland, she insisted she would not permit any interference with her own personal faith, under pain of death. Knox found his powers greatly increased, and he organized the arrest and imprisonment of many Catholic priests, including the Archbishop of St Andrews. Later on, when the marriage to Darnley was imminent, he even went so far as to attack the queen and her intended marriage to a 'papist' in a sermon, and was summoned to answer to her for his audacity. At first Mary eagerly tried to win Knox's friendship and esteem, but his response was so violent and dismissive that she was reduced to tears.

It was soon proposed that Mary marry Elizabeth's favourite, the Earl of Leicester, and this would have led her to be acknowledged as the next heir to the throne of England, since Elizabeth had declared she intended to 'live and die a virgin Queen'. Mary promised to abide entirely by the will of 'her good sister the Queen', but while these negotiations were progressing, Henry, Lord Darnley, the son of the Earl of Lennox, came to Scotland to visit his father. Being a near relative of the two queens and next in succession to the throne, he naturally took an early opportunity to be presented to Mary.

Shortly afterwards, when Elizabeth withdrew her proposal of the marriage to Leicester, Mary, with the same sense of amorous adventure that had characterized her father, her grandfather and her grandmother, made marriage plans of her own which she thought would satisfy all parties.

During the troubles that had occurred soon after Mary's birth, Matthew, Earl of Lennox – regarded with suspicion by both the Protestants and the Catholics in Scotland – took refuge in England, where Henry VIII allowed him to marry his niece, Lady Margaret Douglas. Princess Margaret, the eldest daughter of Henry VII, had married the Earl of Angus on the death of her first husband, James IV, and Lady

Margaret was their daughter. Lennox, belonging to the House of Stuart, was related to the royal family of Scotland, and his wife – apart from the children of Henry VIII and the direct line of succession by her mother's first husband, James IV, which led to Mary – was the legal heir to the crown of England. The first child of this marriage died in infancy, but the second, Henry Stuart, Lord Darnley, was born in 1546, about four years after Mary. This disparity in age, although unfortunate, did not rule out an alliance between the two, in whose veins flowed so much of the blood of the Stuarts and the Tudors.

Along with his niece's hand, Henry VIII had granted Lennox English lands giving a yearly revenue of 1500 marks. Lennox's own estates in Scotland had been forfeited, so he came to be considered more an English than a Scottish subject, but he had long nurtured a secret hope of restoring his fortunes in his native land. Lady Lennox, an ambitious and conniving woman, persuaded him to educate Darnley with a view to seeking marriage with the Scottish queen, and on the death of Francis II she went to Paris to try to ingratiate herself with Mary and promote Darnley as a suitor. Mary probably gave her some encouragement, for few were more sincerely overjoyed at the queen's safe arrival in Scotland than Lady Lennox, who fell on her knees and thanked God that the Scottish queen had escaped the English ships. For her impudence, Cecil sent her to prison for a number of months.

Seeing the difficulties that stood in the way of all her other suitors, in 1564 Mary began to entertain the idea of a marriage with Darnley. Their heir would unite the rival claims of the Stuarts and the Tudors to the English succession, in the absence of issue by Elizabeth, and would give Scotland a native prince of the old royal line. It was difficult to see what reasonable objections could be made to such an alliance. So that she might judge for herself, Mary granted the Earl of Lennox permission to return to Scotland in 1564, after an exile of twenty years, and promised to help him reclaim his hereditary rights.

Although Elizabeth was well aware of the ultimate purpose of this journey, and certainly had no desire to assist it, she did not oppose it. With her usual insight she calculated that much discord and jealousy would arise out of Lennox's attempt to seek favour for his son. She knew that the House of Hamilton, whose claims to the Scottish crown were publicly recognized, regarded the Lennox family as its worst enemies, and that the haughty nobility of Scotland would be unwilling to see a stripling elevated above them all. Besides, the principal estates of Lennox now lay in England, and Elizabeth hoped she could keep control of negotiations and play the same game of trickery and delay she had planned if her recommendation of Leicester had been more favourably received.

Towards the end of 1564 Parliament restored Lennox's estates and honours. The Earl of Argyll surrendered Lennox's possessions, which had passed to him, with extreme reluctance. The Duke of Chatelherault, dreading the marriage with Darnley, remained obstinate in his hatred. So did Mary's illegitimate brother, Lord James Stewart, the Earl of Moray, aware that this new connection would be a fatal blow to his influence, but 'Secretary' Maitland, William Maitland of Lethington, who felt that he had been stifled by Argyll as Prime Minister, did not regret the end of his ascendancy. The Secretary and most of the other members of the Privy Council were courted by Lennox. He gave valuable jewels to them and the queen, but to Moray, whose enmity he knew, he gave nothing. However, Moray's influence in the government had not yet decreased, and to gratify the Protestants he pushed through an Act in that year's Parliament making the attending of mass, except in the queen's chapel, punishable with loss of goods, lands and life. Despite Mary's intercession, the Archbishop of St Andrews, who had infringed this Act, was imprisoned for some months.

Early in 1565, Elizabeth granted leave for Darnley to set out for Scotland. His ostensible purpose was to visit his father and to see the estates to which he had been recently restored, but it was no secret that his real aim was to try to gain favour with Mary. The jealous Elizabeth had a devious plan to provoke a quarrel between Mary and both her own nobility and the English. She recommended Darnley and his father to Mary and gave no hint of her suspicions about the projected alliance. As soon as Mary's intentions were clear, however, Elizabeth would pretend the greatest indignation and claim that the marriage plans had been devised and carried out in secret, hoping either to break off the match altogether or to make Mary's nuptial couch anything but a bed of roses.

Darnley hurried to Edinburgh in a severe snowstorm, only to find that Mary was at Wemyss Castle in Fife, and his father urged him to hurry there immediately. Exaggerated accounts have been given of Mary's first impressions of Darnley, even claiming that it was love at first sight. True, she received him warmly, as someone she wished to like, but she was too accustomed to admiration to surrender her heart at first glance and would have to be wooed. She was no doubt glad that Darnley was one of the handsomest young men of the day, saying playfully that 'he was the lustiest and best proportioned long man she had seen'. She might have said a good deal more, for he was very graceful, with agreeably regular features and an animated face lit up by a pair of dazzling eyes. His riding and dancing were unrivalled, and – probably to curry favour with Mary, who could read in six languages, collected Italian and French poetry, was a good singer and could play a number of musical instruments – he professed a great fondness for poetry and music.

Darnley's exterior was of only secondary interest to Mary and her subjects, however: his mind and character were much more important. His religious convictions seemed ambivalent, and although his mother was a Catholic, he was a member of the Established Church of England, but he saw the need to ingratiate himself with the Scottish Reformers, so on his very first Sunday in Edinburgh he went to hear John Knox preach.

Darnley's great misfortune was that he was inexperienced and immature. He was headstrong, with a violent temper that might have been tamed by hardship but was made all the worse by his sudden rise to eminence. He was passionately fond of power but was unable to make proper use of it. Conscious of his inability to cope with talented people, he gathered round him those who were willing to flatter him on account of his rank or to join him in all kinds of dubious pastimes. He knew something about the duties of a courtier, but he was profoundly ignorant of those of a politician. His polished manners gained him friends at first, but his tendency to jump to conclusions and his ill-grounded prejudices soon converted them into enemies, as in one instance when he deeply offended the Earl of Moray by remarking to one of his brothers that his lands were 'too extensive'. Mary begged Darnley to be more guarded in future. She hoped that time would improve him, but she did not know all his faults yet because he had naturally tried to display only his virtues.

He had been at court about a month before he proposed to Mary. At first she gave him scant encouragement, telling him she had not yet made up her mind and refusing to accept the ring he offered her. Darnley, with his father's assistance, sought powerful support for his cause. His friend, Sir James Melville, spoke in his favour to Mary, as did all the lords who hated or feared Moray, including the Earls of Atholl and Caithness, and the Lords Ruthven and Hume. An even more useful agent was David Rizzio, the queen's Private Secretary, whose abilities she respected. Rizzio's influence with Mary aroused hatred in Moray and others of the Privy Council, so he was pleased to find himself sought after by her future husband.

When the queen and her court were at Stirling in April 1565, a bout of illness also acted in Darnley's favour. At first supposed to be a common cold, a few days later it turned out to be the measles, and Mary tended him through his illness and a subsequent bout of ague.

While Mary was preoccupied with Darnley, the Earl of Bothwell, an acquaintance of Mary's from her time in France who had served in her first Privy Council but been banished to England in 1562 for allegedly plotting to kidnap the queen, returned to Scotland. His misdemeanours were not yet forgotten, and the queen and Moray summoned him to trial in Edinburgh. Unwilling to entrust himself to his ancient enemies, he again left the country for six months, but not before uttering violent threats against Moray and Maitland and speaking so disrespectfully of the queen that she declared he would never receive her favour.

By now Mary had decided to marry Darnley, and sent Maitland to London to inform Elizabeth and ask for her approval. This was the last thing Elizabeth intended to give, and Mary had played right into her hands. She assembled her Privy Council, and at the instigation of Cecil they gave their unanimous opinion that 'this marriage with my Lord Darnley appeared to be unmeet, unprofitable, and directly prejudicial to the sincere amity between both the queens'. The reasons for this decision were revealed in an official paper drawn up by Cecil himself. He did not think the proposed marriage 'meet or profitable' because it would have pleased those who championed Mary's succession to the English throne. Furthermore, representing it as 'dangerous' would allow Mary's enemies to join Elizabeth in opposing it. Cecil had detailed plans for how Mary was to be harassed: they would claim that the leading Catholics in France, including the Houses of Guise and Lorraine, and those Scottish Catholics who hated the Duke of Chatelherault, the Hamiltons, Moray and the Reformers approved of the marriage; a rumour was to be spread that some of Mary and Darnley's friends would try to alienate Elizabeth's subjects and even attempt take her life, and finally, unrest and rebellions in Scotland were to be fomented in secret.

Elizabeth sent Sir Nicolas Throckmorton to Scotland to inform Mary of the decision. Arriving at Stirling on 15 May 1565, in an audience with Mary he set forth Elizabeth's disapproval and disallowance of 'the hasty proceeding with my Lord Darnley'. Mary replied that she was sorry Elizabeth disliked the match, but that she had never asked the English queen's permission – she had only informed her of the person she had chosen to marry. She expressed surprise at Elizabeth's opposition, since the English Resident at her court, Randolph, had informed her that as long as she avoided a foreign alliance, 'she might take her choice of any person within the realms of England or Scotland, without any exception'. She had chosen Darnley because she had thought that his royal blood relationship with both her and Elizabeth made him the ideal suitor.

Convinced that Mary would not change her mind, Throckmorton wrote to Elizabeth that the only way she could stop the marriage was to resort to violence. Elizabeth was too prudent to do this herself, especially when others could be persuaded to do so on her behalf. Accordingly, she ordered Throckmorton, one of her wiliest diplomatic agents, to contact the Scottish malcontents, especially the Earl of Moray, and assure them of Elizabeth's support if they chose to take extreme measures. Moray was also invited to correspond with Cecil, which he willingly did. To give the whole affair as serious an air as possible, a fresh supply of troops was sent to the Earl of Bedford, Elizabeth's Lieutenant of the Borders, and her Wardens of the Marches were commanded to show no more favour to Mary's subjects than simply abstaining from any breach of the peace. The Earl of Northumberland, who was attached to the Lennox family, was arrested in London, and Lady Lennox herself was committed to the Tower of London. Lady Somerset, who pretended a sort of title to the English succession in opposition to Mary, was received very graciously at the court of Westminster. Secretary Maitland was induced to associate himself with Moray and the other discontents. Meanwhile, to avoid suspicion on the Continent of such an insidious plot towards Mary, overtures were made to France and Spain.

Elizabeth next wrote letters to Lennox and Darnley, commanding them both, as her subjects, to return to England without delay. Randolph was instructed to wait for their answer. He received little satisfaction from either – Lennox firmly refused to obey and Darnley responded with contempt. Randolph then sought Mary's view. She was deeply angered by Elizabeth's action and received Randolph with greater reserve than ever before. When he asked if she would give Lennox and Darnley permission to depart for England, Mary smiled and said: 'If I would give them leave, I doubt what they would do themselves. I see no will in them to return.' Randolph replied insolently that if they refused, and were supported by Mary in that refusal, Elizabeth had the power and the will to seek revenge. Mary merely replied that she hoped Elizabeth would change her mind, and dismissed him.

Mary then sent John Hay to the English court to state once more her wish to avoid giving any offence to Elizabeth, but at the same time to repeat that she could not understand her opposition to the marriage. He was also to complain of the 'sharp handling' that had been given to Mary's aunt, Lady Margaret Douglas, Countess of Lennox. But her chief anxieties arose from matters nearer home. The Duke of Chatelherault and the Earls of Moray, Argyll and Glencairn had openly declared their opposition to the marriage, and Maitland of Lethington and Morton were suspected of giving it only very doubtful support, so there were great changes at Mary's court. Those who formerly had most influence kept away from it altogether, and a new set of men unaccustomed to state duties, including Montrose, Fleming, Cassillis and Montgomery, came into favour. Mary turned to Rizzio, who was active, well acquainted with all the details of public business and was liked by Darnley.

CHAPTER

II

*M*ARRIAGE AND REBELLION

Moray and his associates were keen to serve both Elizabeth's and their own interests by doing all they could to prevent the marriage, and she gave them every encouragement. She wrote letters to the conspirators' leaders, there were efforts to win over the General Assembly, which met in June 1565, to their views, and the nobles summoned by Mary to a convention at Perth were lobbied for support. Nevertheless, the great majority at the convention consented to and approved of the proposed marriage.

Moray, in despair, begged Randolph to inform Elizabeth that he and his faction had decided to foment a rebellion to prevent Darnley from obtaining the crown and, if an opportunity arose, to imprison Mary and rule the country themselves. This was exactly what Elizabeth had been trying to promote in Scotland. Randolph realized that many approved of the imprisonment of the Countess of Lennox and would be happy to see her husband and son join her. Since it was felt that there must be plausible grounds for such an extreme act, Moray claimed that there had been a conspiracy to assassinate him at the Perth convention. His story was that one of his own servants and another man supported by the retainers of Atholl and Lennox had quarrelled, and it had been arranged that they should renew their dispute at Perth, when Moray was to be slain in the ensuing affray. However, the only evidence of a plot against him was Moray's own statement, and when Mary asked him to supply details in writing, knowing that he was using it as an excuse for refusing to come to court, his story proved doubtful.

The treasonable views of Moray and his friends are subject to no such doubt. In those times the usual way to secure a change of government was to abduct the sovereign, and this was Moray's ultimate intention. On Sunday 1 July 1565 the queen was to ride with Darnley and a small party of friends from Perth to the seat of Lord Livingston at Callander, to attend the baptism of one of his children. Moray knew that her journey would take her through several steep, wild passes where the party could easily be overpowered. Knox reported that the rugged path of Dron, about three miles south of Perth, had been mentioned as the intended location for the attack, while others claim it was the Kirk of Beith, which stood on an isolated piece of ground between Dunfermline and Queensferry.

However, late on the Saturday night a rumour of the plot reached Mary. To prevent it she ordered the Earl of Atholl and Lord Ruthven to gather together as many men as possible, and she left Perth at 5 a.m. on Sunday, accompanied by three hundred horsemen. Moray was waiting at Loch Leven, Argyll at Castle Campbell, Chatelherault at his house of Kinneil near Queensferry and Lord Rothes was at the nearby Parrot Well, but the queen travelled past their intended ambush point both much earlier in the day and much more strongly guarded than they had anticipated – indeed, the Earl of Argyll did not join Moray until two hours after Mary had ridden through Kinross.

On Mary's return to Edinburgh she found that Knox and Moray had been attempting to stir up sedition among some of the more bigoted Presbyterians by claiming that Darnley favoured Catholicism. Two or three hundred of the malcontents (or 'brethren', as Knox called them) assembled at St Leonard's Hill, and there might have been ugly scenes if Mary had not arrived just in time to disperse and overawe them. Moray and his associates, keeping well out of the way, held some secret meetings at Loch Leven and then assembled at Stirling on 17 July to declare open rebellion.

Despite all these troubles, Mary, conscious that she had right on her side, remained undaunted and at no period of her life was her strength of mind more apparent. To retain the confidence that the great majority of her subjects still had in her, she issued proclamations announcing that she would continue to abstain from any interference in religious matters. She wrote letters to many of her nobles assuring them of the integrity of her intentions, and she called on all those loyal to her to collect and arm their followers and come to her assistance.

The Earl of Moray, on the other hand, having betrayed his own queen, became entirely subservient to the wishes and commands of Elizabeth. He and his friends wrote to ask her to send them £3,000 to meet the expenses of the current year, and they felt this would ensure their success unless Mary received foreign assistance. They also suggested that

Lord Hume, who had estates in the Borders and was one of Mary's most faithful servants, should be harassed by some 'accidental' incursions, that the Bishop of Dunblane, who was being sent as an ambassador to the Continent, should be delayed in London until 'his budgets were rifled by some good slight or other', and that Bothwell, whom Mary was about to recall to assist her, should be 'kept in good surety' for a time. To all this Elizabeth replied that if Moray and his cohort encountered any difficulties, 'they should not find lack in her to succour them'. However, she hinted that the less money they asked for the better, advising them 'neither to make greater expense than their security makes necessary, nor less which may bring danger'.

Since returning from France, Mary's conduct had been exemplary, her only fault, forced on her by circumstances, being that she had followed her brother's advice too closely. In some instances his counsel had been judicious, and in others his natural severity had been tempered by Mary's mildness, with the result that her government was the most popular Scotland had ever known and her choice of Darnley as husband was greeted with widespread approval. To secure the political advantages that her country would gain from this alliance, she was willing to forgo much more splendid offers, and although Darnley may not have been perfect, his stature made him an ideal father for her offspring. Nor could his religious opinions raise objections, for, whatever they were, they did not influence the queen – indeed, ever since she had met him she had treated the Protestants with even more than her usual liberality. At the baptism of Lord Livingston's child she stayed to listen to a Protestant sermon, and about the same time she told some of the leaders of the Reformers that although she remained loyal to her own religion, she would nevertheless allow a conference and debate on the scriptures in her presence, and also a public sermon by Mr Erskine of Dun, whom she regarded as 'a mild and sweet-natured man, with true honesty and uprightness'.

In such circumstances it is difficult to conceive how, even in those restless times, anyone dared to envisage a rebellion against Mary. The answer can be found in the selfish scheming of Elizabeth, the jealousy of the Duke of Chatelherault, whose family held the succession to the Scottish crown and who had hoped that his son, Arran, might have married Mary, the envy and rage of the Earl of Argyll, who had been obliged to surrender to Lennox some of his forfeited estates, and above all the artful, grasping spirit of Moray. Whatever one may think of Mary's subsequent conduct, it is apparent that the first serious troubles of her reign were no fault of her own but were the result of intrigues by enemies who were all the more dangerous because they had once appeared to be friends.

Whatever the conspirators' hopes or wishes, Mary decided that their desire to prevent her marriage should not be allowed to serve as a pretext for continued insurrection. On Sunday 29 July 1565 she married Darnley, on whom she had previously conferred various titles, including Duke of Albany. The banns were read in the Canongate Church, the Palace of Holyrood being in that parish, and as Mary and Darnley were first cousins, a dispensation had been obtained from the Pope. The Catholic ceremony was performed by John Sinclair, Dean of Restalrig and Bishop of Brechin, in the chapel of Holyrood between 5 and 6 a.m. It was re-marked that a handsomer couple had never been seen in Scotland. Mary was now twenty-three and at the very height of her beauty, and Darnley, although only nineteen, was very manly for his age.

The festivities may not have matched the grandeur of Mary's first wedding – the Scots had less elegant tastes than the French, and in those troubled times it was necessary for an armed guard to stand round the altar – but nevertheless, in front of a great congregation of lords and ladies, Mary, in a flowing black robe with a wide mourning hood, was led to the altar by the Earls of Lennox and Atholl who then brought in the bridegroom. Once the Bishop had united them, three rings were placed on the queen's finger – the middle one a rich diamond. They then knelt together, and many prayers were said over them. Finally, Darnley kissed his bride, and as he was not himself Catholic, left her in the chapel to hear mass.

Afterwards, most of the company followed her to her apartments, where she laid aside her sable garments to indicate that from now on she would forget her grief at the loss of her first husband. In observance of an old custom, as many of the lords as could approach near enough were allowed to assist in disrobing her by taking out a pin. Her ladies then dressed her in magnificent robes and brought her to the ball-room, where there was great cheer and dancing until dinner-time. At dinner Darnley appeared in his royal robes, and after a great flourish of trumpets, gifts were distributed to the great crowds that surrounded the palace. The Earls of Atholl, Morton and Crawford attended the queen as sewer, carver and cup-bearer, and the Earls of Eglinton, Cassilis and Glen-cairn performed the same duties for Darnley. When dinner was over, the dancing was renewed until suppertime, after which the company retired for the night.

The rejoicings that attended the beginning of Darnley's career as King of Scotland were short-lived, however. Randolph expressed the sentiments of Elizabeth and the rebels when he said: 'God must either send the King a short end, or them a miserable life; that either he must be taken away, or they find some support, that what he intendeth to others may light upon himself.'

Moray had now gone too far to turn back, although had he chosen to do so, Mary would no doubt have been willing to show him leniency. John Hay, her former ambassador in England and a friend of her brother's, was sent to Moray to declare that both the Earl of Lennox and Darnley wished him well, and Mary even declared that she was prepared to try anyone who had conspired to murder him, but he had no evidence for his false accusations.

Via Randolph, Elizabeth now sent even more imperative orders than before for the return of Lennox and Darnley, but Lennox replied that since his wife had been committed to the Tower unjustly, he thought it unlikely that the English climate would suit his constitution. Darnley boldly and gallantly said that he now acknowledged duty and obedience to none but the Queen of Scots, and although Elizabeth chose to envy his good fortune, he saw no reason why he should leave a country where he was so comfortable. Randolph coolly replied that he hoped to see the downfall of all those who were of the same mind and left unceremoniously.

As soon as the disaffected Scottish lords heard of Mary's marriage and the proclamation of Darnley as king, they renewed their complaints with increased bitterness. The majority of their countrymen saw through their real motives, however, even Knox acknowledging that it was generally held that their complaints were 'not for religion, but rather for hatred, envy of sudden promotion or dignity, or such worldly causes'. The recall of the Earls of Bothwell and Sutherland and the restoration of Lord Gordon to the forfeited estates and honours of his father, the Earl of Huntly, also caused exasperation, but Mary knew she could depend upon these noblemen, although she did not like Bothwell personally.

A message that Elizabeth sent to Mary early in August 1565, and Mary's reply, underline the total groundlessness of Elizabeth's and the Scottish rebels' complaints against Mary at this time. The message was brought by Tamworth, one of Elizabeth's inferior officials, an insolent man who was specially chosen to convey Elizabeth's disrespect. He was ordered not to acknowledge Darnley as king and to address him only by his English title. Mary refused to see him in person, however, since she had an inkling of Elizabeth's intentions, so his objections were conveyed in writing, as was Mary's reply.

The message stated that Elizabeth had found Mary's recent conduct, both towards Elizabeth and her subjects, very odd, for various reasons. Mary replied to each accusation point by point.

Elizabeth swore that her offer to Mary of any of her own subjects in marriage was made sincerely and lovingly, and that she was grieved to hear that Mary, listening to false counsel, had been made to think otherwise. Mary answered that she did not doubt Elizabeth's sincerity in her offer of a husband from England and that no counsel had been given to induce her to change her opinion.

Elizabeth was very surprised that despite Mary's offer to Throckmorton to delay her marriage until the middle of August to allow more time to seek Elizabeth's consent, she had married on 29 July without giving her any notice, disappointing both Elizabeth and some foreign princes, who also thought the alliance strange. Mary replied it was true that she had decided to marry Darnley before Throckmorton came into Scotland, but she had promised to delay her marriage in the hope that Elizabeth's doubts about its propriety might be overcome. However, this promise was made on the express condition that commissioners were appointed by both sides to discuss the matter, and Elizabeth's refusal to nominate any commissioners meant that Mary was no longer bound by her promise. Furthermore, she had good reasons, which were nobody else's business, for marrying Darnley when she did. With regard to certain foreign princes thinking the alliance 'strange', she had sought the opinions and obtained the express consent and approval of the greatest princes in Christendom.

Elizabeth was astonished that Mary, in direct contravention of the peace treaty between England and Scotland, had detained Elizabeth's subjects, Lennox and Darnley, in Scotland, having lured them there under the pretence of pursuing suits for lands but in reality to form an alliance without Elizabeth's consent – an offence so unnatural that it had provoked widespread disapproval and Elizabeth could not forget it. Mary declared that she marvelled at Elizabeth, her sister, responding in this way: how could it be thought strange for her to 'detain' within her realm the person she had married, or a Scottish earl appointed to his Scottish title by Elizabeth herself, especially since they both came with Elizabeth's consent and letters of recommendation? She had no doubt that the world judged that her conduct was in no way prejudicial to any peace treaty between the two realms, since no annoyance was intended towards Elizabeth, her kingdom or estate.

Elizabeth was surprised that Mary's ambassador, John Hay, had been sent to enquire about Elizabeth's objections to the marriage and what she wished to be done but had been granted no authority either to agree to or refuse her requests. She therefore assumed that he had been sent more out of empty form than for any useful purpose. Mary responded that although she was willing to hear Elizabeth's objections, if she had any, and to try to remedy them, she had declared that she would only do this through mutually agreed commissioners. She was so convinced of the suitability of the marriage, however, that even now she was still willing, if Elizabeth wished, to have its propriety discussed by such commissioners.

Elizabeth asked for an explanation of a sentence in one of Mary's letters written in French, which she found somewhat ambiguous: '*Je n'estimerois jamais que cela vienne de vous, et sans en chercher autre vengeance, j'aurois recours à tous les princes mes alliés pour avec moi vous remonstrer ce que je vous suis par parentage. Vous savez assez ce que vous avez resolu sur cela.*' Mary replied that the whole of her letter, as well as the passage in question, simply expressed her desire to remain on friendly terms with Elizabeth, from whom she expected such treatment as was appropriate from one princess to another who was her relative, and that if – God forbid – less favourable treatment were received, she would have no option but to lay her case before other princes, her friends and allies.

Elizabeth was aggrieved to see that Mary harboured fugitives and offenders from England, had practised deception in Elizabeth's realm and that in her own kingdom, seduced by false counsellors and malicious information, she had raised up factions among the nobility. Mary answered that if she really wished to offend Elizabeth, she would not be content with such paltry practices as those she was accused of towards English subjects. With regard to her proceedings in her own realm, just as she had never interfered with Elizabeth's government, believing it wrong for one state to meddle in the internal affairs of another, she requested Elizabeth not to meddle with hers but to trust Mary to preserve the peace.

Elizabeth warned Mary to not to proceed in her intention to suppress and extirpate the religion already established in Scotland nor to try to suppress the Reformed faith in England, since any such designs would rebound on those who advised and engaged in them. Mary could only marvel at Elizabeth's fears for a religion that Mary had never attempted to impede or change, indeed whose establishment had been promoted among her Scottish subjects. As for any intention to interfere with the religion of England, she had never heard of it before, but if any evidence were presented, it would instantly be explained and the cause for alarm addressed. With regard to her 'designs', those she engaged in were no more vain or deceitful than her neighbours'.

Finally, Elizabeth wished that Mary would not be so fickle as to think evil of the Earl of Moray, for there were numerous examples of noblemen being driven to take measures for their own security that they would otherwise never have resorted to, adding that these were *some* of the reasons why Elizabeth was upset with Mary. Mary replied that she wished her good sister would not meddle with the affairs of her Scottish subjects any more than Mary meddled with the affairs of Elizabeth's English subjects. If Elizabeth wanted an explanation of Mary's conduct towards Moray, it would be willingly given – as soon as Elizabeth explained her motives for committing to the Tower Lady Margaret, Countess of Lennox, Mary's mother-in-law and aunt. If Elizabeth would state any *other* grounds for offence, they would be answered just as candidly.

Having thus triumphantly replied to Elizabeth's irritating message, Mary, in the true spirit of conciliation, had the magnanimity to propose that certain articles should be agreed.

On the part of the King and Queen of Scots: 'First, That their Majesties being satisfied of the Queen their sister's friendship, are content to assure the Queen that during the term of her life, or that of her lawful issue, they will not, directly or indirectly, attempt anything prejudicial to their sister's title to the Crown of England, or in any way disturb the quietness of that kingdom. Second, they will enter into no communication with any subject or subjects of the realm of England, in prejudice of their said sister and her lawful issue, or receive into their protection any subjects of the realm of England with whom their sister may have occasion to be offended. Third, they will not enter into any league or confederation with any foreign prince, to the hurt, damage, and displeasure of the Queen and realm of England. Fourth, they will enter into any such league and confederation with the Queen and realm of England as shall be for the weal of the princes and subjects on both sides. And Fifth, they will not go about to procure in any way alteration, innovation, or change in the religion, laws, or liberties of the realm of England, though it should please God at any time hereafter to call them to the succession of that kingdom.'

In return for these offers, the three following equally reasonable articles were to be agreed to on the part of England: 'First, that by Act of Parliament, the succession to the Crown, failing Elizabeth and her lawful issue, shall be established, first, in the person of Mary and her lawful issue, and failing them, in the person of the Countess of Lennox and her lawful issue, as by the law of God and nature entitled to the inheritance of the said Crown. Second, that the second offer made by the King and Queen of Scots be also made on the part of England; and Third, that the third offer shall be likewise mutual.'

It would not have suited Elizabeth to agree to these liberal articles, so nothing more was heard of them.

On 15 August 1565 Moray summoned the rebellious nobles to a public meeting at Ayr, where they resolved to assemble bearing arms on 24 August. As a result, Mary issued proclamations calling on her loyal subjects to come to Edinburgh on 25 August with their kin, friends and household, bringing sufficient provisions for fifteen days. On that day she left Edinburgh with a large army and marched to Linlithgow. Before leaving the capital, measures were taken to prevent the discontented there taking advantage of the queen's absence. She sacked the provost, who was a lackey of Knox's and strongly suspected of favouring the rebels, and appointed a more trustworthy civic officer.

A few days earlier, Knox himself had been suspended from clerical duties because of a seditious and insulting sermon he had delivered before the young king, who was paying him the compliment of attending divine service in St Giles's church a Sunday or two after his marriage. In this sermon the preacher, among other things, said that for the sins of the people, God had raised to the throne boys and women, adding, in the words of scripture: 'I will give children to be their princes, and babes shall rule over them: children are their oppressors, and women rule over them.' In the same grossly personal vein, he remarked: 'God justly punished Ahab, because he did not correct his idolatrous wife, the harlot Jezebel.' It is notable that Knox never thought of objecting to Mary's marriage with Darnley until he realized that his patron, Moray, to whom he was now reconciled, did not approve of it. Only a few months earlier, he had declared approvingly of the match: 'Lord Darnley . . . marrieth Queen Mary, King James V's daughter: and so the king's desire is fulfilled, viz. the crown continueth in the name and in the family.'

From Linlithgow, Mary advanced with a growing army, first to Stirling and then to Glasgow. Here she was within a short distance of the rebel army, about twelve hundred strong, which had taken position at Paisley, five miles from Glasgow. Rather than attempting to attack Mary's troops, Moray made a circuit at some distance and arrived unexpectedly at Edinburgh, where he hoped to enlist reinforcements. He was badly disappointed. Finding that the provost, who was taken by surprise, lacked the forces to keep him outside the city walls, Moray entered it by the West Port and immediately dispatched messengers for assistance in every direction and by beat of drum called upon all men who wished to receive wages 'for the defence of the glory of God' to join his standard. Few joined up, and Moray received little support in Edinburgh, although Knox himself did all he could for his patron by means of prayers and exhortations in which he called the rebels 'the best part of the nobility, and chief members of the Congregation'. The public favoured Mary because Moray's real motives were well known.

As soon as the queen was made aware that she had missed her enemies, she marched back in pursuit of them, at the head of five thousand men, as far as Callander. All Moray could do was flee from an army he knew he could not match. Alarmed by Mary's speedy return, he left Edinburgh, dodged her again and led his followers to Lanark and then to Hamilton. With indomitable perseverance, the queen retraced her steps to Glasgow, expecting Moray to attempt to take that city. Finding there was no safety for him in this part of Scotland, however, Moray suddenly turned south and with as little delay as possible retreated into Dumfriesshire. Here, being near the Borders, he expected that Elizabeth would send him aid and he could at any time retreat into England.

The principal noblemen with him were the Duke of Chatelherault, the Earls of Argyll, Glencairn and Rothes, and the Lords Boyd and Ochiltree. Morton and Maitland remained with the queen, but the loyalty of both was suspect, although Boyd was in command of the main body of the royal army. The Earl of Lennox led the vanguard, and the queen, in a suit of light armour, carrying pistols at her saddle-bow, rode with her officers, her courage and stature increasing all the time. She did not think it worthwhile to follow Moray into Dumfriesshire but chose to lead her army through Fife to St Andrews, on the way taking possession of Castle Campbell, the seat of the rebel Lord Argyll.

Meanwhile, Elizabeth was far from inattentive to her servants in Scotland. Randolph wrote to Cecil that if she assisted them with men and more money, the rebels would be able to send Mary to England as a prisoner. The Earl of Bedford informed Elizabeth of her friends' arrival in the Borders and hinted that their cause was not very popular in Scotland and their army was no match for Mary's. Elizabeth's letter in reply is as artful a piece of writing as has ever been produced. Afraid of being seen to be assisting the losing party, she decided to make it appear that she was acting against them, so she wrote to Bedford that in response to representations from him, Randolph and others, she was sending him £3,000, £1,000 of which was to be paid immediately to Moray, in the most private way possible and as if it came from Bedford himself. The remainder was to be kept until it was needed. To the request from Moray and his associates for soldiers, she responded: '. . . though we would not command you to give them aid, yet if we would but wink at your doing herein, and seem to blame you for attempting such things, as you, with the help of others, should bring about . . . we are content, and do authorize you, if you shall see it necessary for their defence, to let them (as of your own adventure, and without notification that you have any direction therein from us), to have the number of 300 soldiers. . . . And so we assure you, our conscience moveth us to charge you so to proceed with them; and yet we would not that either of these were known to be our act, but rather to be covered with your own desire and attempt.'

Having mentioned that she had recently written to Mary to assure her of her esteem and goodwill, Elizabeth boldly affixed her signature to this memorable record of unblushing duplicity.

But Mary was not to be lulled into false security. At St Andrews she issued a proclamation exposing the hollowness of the grounds on which arms had been taken up against her and showing that religion was only a cover for more ungodly designs. Referring in particular to Moray, on whom she had bestowed so many benefits, this proclamation laid bare his ambition to continue to have the queen and the whole realm in his own hands, to be used and governed as he wished: 'By letters sent from themselves to us, they make plain profession that the establishment of religion will not content them, but we must per force be governed by such council as it shall please them to appoint unto us. The like was never demanded of any our most noble progenitors heretofore, yea, not even of governors or regents; but the prince, or such as occupied his place, ever chose his council of such as he thought most fit for the purpose. When we ourselves were of less age, and at our first arrival in our realm, we had free choice of our council at our pleasure; and now, when we are at our full majority, shall we be brought back to the state of pupils and minors, or be put under tutelage? So long as some of them bore the whole swing with us themselves, this matter was never called in question; but now, when they cannot be longer permitted to do and undo all things of their appetite, they will put a bridle in our mouths, and give us a council chosen after their phantasy! To speak it in plain language, they would be king themselves; or at the least, leaving to us the bare name and title, take to themselves the whole use and administration of the kingdom.'

After levying a small fine of 200 marks from the town of Dundee, which had given some help to the malcontents, Mary and Darnley returned to Edinburgh. The news they received there of the increasing strength of the rebels made them decide to march southwards. Biggar was named as the rendezvous for the lieges, and they flocked in such crowds to join their queen's standard that Mary was able to advance towards the Borders at the head of an army of eighteen thousand men. Before this greatly superior force, Moray and his partisans, including his three hundred English soldiers, withdrew to Carlisle with the royal army in close pursuit. His troops dispersed, and he and his friends had to flee farther into England. After visiting Lochmaben Castle, Mary left Bothwell with some troops to watch the Borders and on 18 October returned to Edinburgh with the rest of her army.

Of the rebellious nobles forced into exile, Chatelherault alone was able or willing to make his peace immediately. He and his sons were pardoned, on condition that they lived abroad – a degree of leniency extended to them against the wishes of the House of Lennox, which was anxious for the total ruin of the Hamiltons. Moray and the rest, being received with kindness by Bedford, settled at Newcastle, and Moray and the Abbot of Kilwinning were deputed to inform Elizabeth of the state of affairs. However, Elizabeth had no intention of showing them friendship in adversity. As soon as she heard that Moray was on his way, she wrote to tell him to stay away and to inform him that it was unwise for him to have any 'open dealing' with her.

Bedford intervened on his behalf, and he was allowed to continue his journey, to make some proposals for the 'common cause', but it was a long while before he was granted an audience with the queen. When they finally met, she had the audacity to ask him how he, a rebel against her sister queen, dared be so bold as to enter her realm. Moray tried to protest that she had supported him all along. Fearful of betraying her schemes to her Continental neighbours, Elizabeth declared exasperatedly that Moray and his friends would never obtain anything from her but scorn and neglect unless he made a public recantation. Both Moray and the abbot had little choice but to comply, and although Throckmorton backed them up by asserting that he had been sent into Scotland expressly to offer assistance to the rebels, he could not save them from the degradation Elizabeth inflicted.

When they appeared before her, she was surrounded by the French and Spanish ambassadors. They were made to kneel and take an oath that Elizabeth had never incited them to rebel against their own queen. As soon as they had uttered this falsehood, Elizabeth said to them: 'Now ye have told the truth; for neither did I, nor any in my name, stir you up against your Queen. Your abominable treason may serve for example to my own subjects to rebel against me. Therefore, get ye out of my presence; ye are but unworthy traitors.'

The deputation returned quite crestfallen to their friends at Newcastle, where they lived for some time in great poverty and misery. These were the more immediate results of this piece of juggling on the part of Elizabeth and Moray's justly unsuccessful rebellion.

CHAPTER III

𝒯HE EARL OF MORTON'S PLOT

Until now, Mary's government had been prosperous and popular. There had been numerous difficulties, but she had overcome them so successfully that her sovereignty was secure. However, Mary's marriage to Darnley was to continue to cause problems, and the banishment of the majority of her most experienced counsellors along with the Earl of Moray and the Hamiltons had left her government weakened. At the head of those who remained was the crafty Earl of Morton, who, although outwardly loyal, secretly longed for the return of his old allies among the Protestant faction.

The Reformists had good reasons for concern. Darnley now openly supported Catholicism, the most powerful of the Lords of the Congregation were in disgrace, several of the Catholic nobility had been restored to their honours, and Mary had allowed some of the Catholic ecclesiastics to return to Parliament. Furthermore, ambassadors from the King of France and Mary's Continental friends were advising her to grant no terms to the exiled nobles and were encouraging her to support the Holy League. Instigated by Catherine de Medici, Mary's former mother-in-law, and the Duke of

Alva, this alliance had recently been formed at Bayonne between Charles IX of France and his sister, the Queen of Spain, with the consent of her husband, Philip, and Pope Pius IV to suppress the Reformation throughout Europe by any means necessary.

Although these circumstances were naturally alarming to Protestants, Mary's intentions, which were not known at the time, remain in doubt to this day. It is extremely doubtful that Mary ever gave either her consent or approval to the League. She certainly had the intention of securing 'something for the ease of Catholics' in the next parliament, but this was only to be a request for the Protestants to be more tolerant. As for the Bayonne confederacy, since it resolved 'by treachery and circumvention, by fire and the sword, utterly to exterminate the Protestants over Christendom', it is highly unlikely that Mary would have supported it – the civil war and confusion it was bound to provoke would have weakened her own position, set her against the majority of her subjects and would hardly have improved her chances of succession to the English crown.

Although there is no proof that Mary contemplated the subversion of Reformism in Scotland, she was uncertain how to deal with the exiled rebels. Elizabeth petitioned on their behalf, knowing she could depend on their co-operation as soon as they were back in power, and this was welcomed by Moray's friends in Scotland – some for religious reasons, many for their own private interests, and a few because they believed his return would be good for the country. On the other hand, the Catholics were delighted to be rid of such formidable adversaries, and their feelings were shared by Mary's uncle, the Cardinal of Lorraine. For her own part, although Mary could be lenient almost to a fault, she must have felt just indignation against those who had so grossly abused her kindness and subverted her authority.

Against this background, a parliament was summoned, first meeting on 4 February 1566 and then prorogued until 7 March, which determined that the issue had to be resolved in one way or another. Its decision would almost certainly have been unfavourable to Moray if there had not been unexpected developments.

Mary and Darnley had been married only a few months when she began to realize that she had made a mistake by uniting her fortunes with such a weak, headstrong and inexperienced youth. During their courtship, Darnley's apparent devotion to Mary and his care in hiding his numerous character defects had won her heart and – even more important to him – a share in her throne, but as soon as he succeeded in his aim, he showed his true colours. He broke out into a thousand excesses, offended almost all the nobility and, forgetting – or misunderstanding – the kind of men he was dealing with, cherished a wild and boyish desire to make his own will law. Although he had converted from Protestantism to Catholicism, the Catholics had no confidence in him, whereas Knox and the Reformers were furious and alarmed by his action. He behaved like a playboy and was more interested in his hounds and hawks than affairs of state. He was also a heavy drinker, and on one occasion, attending a civic banquet with the queen, he flared up at her so brutally that she left in tears.

It was not only Darnley's character that began to alienate

him from Mary, however. It would be wrong to say that there was rivalry between them, for this would place Mary on equal terms with her husband – she was queen in her own right, while Darnley had no entitlement to any authority beyond what she chose to confer on him. In the early days of their marriage, her loving loyalty repeatedly led her to let him have his own way, and he was too conceited and selfish to appreciate the trust she placed in him. Darnley refused to listen to the prudent advice of Sir James Melville and others she asked him to associate with and was incapable of understanding Mary's proud spirit. If he had continued to show her the affection she was due, she would have granted him every honour he desired, but once he began to slight her, nothing he could do would force her to grant his wishes.

On the day that Mary gave her hand to Darnley, she conferred on him the title King of Scotland. In public writs his name was sometimes signed before, sometimes after, her own, and coins of the realm issued after the marriage carried his name as well as hers. Mary never intended to surrender to him greater influence in the administration than her own, however, and this was Darnley's dearest ambition. To achieve it, he demanded the 'crown matrimonial' under the Scottish code. In its more limited sense, if a man married a woman of superior rank he was vested with equal power and rank to her as long as their marriage lasted. But Darnley wanted to extend the terms of this convention. Knowing that the laws of Scotland held that a man who married an heiress should possess her estate not only during his wife's life but until his own death, he was anxious to continue as sovereign even if Mary died without issue. In the first throes of her love for Darnley, Mary might have been willing, with the consent of parliament, to grant his wishes, but as soon as he revealed himself to be unstable and dissipated, she felt obliged to refuse, both for her own sake and that of the country.

The more Mary opposed him, the more determined Darnley became to have his own way. Mary's Private Secretary, the Catholic David Rizzio, one of her most faithful servants, had approved of her marriage to Darnley for political reasons. This had won him the hatred of Moray and his allies, and the friendship and support of Darnley. But Rizzio was too fond of Mary to wish to see her husband become her master. He may also have had personal motives: he knew he was a favourite of Mary's and would keep his place at court as long as she prevailed, but he had developed serious doubts about Darnley. As a result the two men's friendship cooled, and the consideration Mary continued to show Rizzio only made matters worse.

At this point the Earl of Morton, secretly supported by Maitland, and more openly by Lords Ruthven and Lindsay, decided to try to harness Darnley's discontent to promote the interests of himself and some of his political allies. He aimed to strengthen his party's representation in parliament by securing the return of Moray, Argyll, Rothes and the other banished lords, which would help to prevent Mary's attempts to push through Acts to restore to her ecclesiastics some church lands that he and others had taken unlawfully. Mary naturally had no intention of pardoning Moray and the rebels, but Rizzio was almost alone among her ministers in supporting her decision, and he stood his ground both on this issue and that of the crown matrimonial, despite open threats from Darnley, intrigue by Morton and an attempt at bribery by Moray.

Scotland was therefore divided into four powerful factions, headed by Mary, Morton, Darnley and Moray. As long as Mary held power, the other three factions had little hope of success, so they formed a coalition and hatched a plot with a secrecy and callousness typical of Morton. They drafted and signed a formal set of articles between Henry, King of Scotland, and James, Earl of Moray, Archibald, Earl of Argyll, Andrew, Earl of Rothes, Robert, Lord Boyd, Andrew, Lord Ochiltree and certain others 'remaining in England', which stipulated that at the first parliament held after their return, the lords would secure for Darnley the crown matrimonial and would 'seek, pursue, and extirpate out of the realm of Scotland, or take and slay them' anyone who opposed it – a pointed reference to Mary. In return, Darnley agreed to oppose any proceedings for forfeiture of lands against them and, as soon as he obtained the crown matrimonial, to grant them free remission for all crimes and to remove and punish anyone who opposed it. These articles implied high treason and reveal Darnley's unpardonable disloyalty, both as a husband and as a man.

Morton decided to take advantage of the fact that Mary's recent successes had made her overconfident, so that she did not suspect the plot. It was now February, parliament was to meet on 7 March, and the absent lords were to be tried on 12 March, after which the forfeited church lands would be restored to their rightful owners. But this could be averted if

Mary could be captured, if her principal anti-Protestant ministers could be removed and if Darnley could be installed in supreme command. Parliament might either be prorogued or intimidated into submission. An open attempt to imprison the queen would have been too daring and dangerous, however, so under the pretence of concern for her personal safety and protecting the best interests of the country, she was to be prevented from exercising her own independent authority as long as they thought necessary. Rizzio was to be the scapegoat and first victim of the conspiracy.

Rizzio was hated throughout Scotland, and the Reformers in particular exaggerated his influence on the queen and represented him as the Pope's minion, so it would be a popular move if the plot were presented as seeking to remove him to safeguard the country. As a foreigner, Rizzio had good reason to fear for his safety. Although the appointment of an Italian to the post of Private Secretary had a certain logic since his command of Continental languages was useful, the impression that he was dabbling in Scotland's internal affairs led to general mistrust, and many courtiers openly envied his close relationship with Mary. Melville advised him to ask the queen to avoid showing him favour when others were present, but she would have none of it, and when Melville broached the subject with her himself, she insisted that Rizzio meddled no more in her writings and affairs than her previous secretary had done.

Rizzio's religion was another reason for his great unpopularity. There were rumours that he was in the pay of the Pope and was in close correspondence with the Cardinal of Lorraine. Whatever the truth, in those bigoted times his support for the Scottish Catholics was enough to condemn him.

Finally, there is evidence that Rizzio, whom Morton recognized as an intelligent and formidable adversary, not only refused to take part in the conspiracy to abduct Mary but even revealed the plot to her when he discovered Ruthven and the other conspirators, including Darnley, meeting in secret in a small room in the palace.

Nevertheless, on the evening of Saturday 9 March 1566, nearly five hundred armed retainers of the treasonous lords assembled secretly near the Palace of Holyrood, and when darkness fell, Morton, as Lord High Chancellor, led them into the interior courtyard without encountering much difficulty or arousing much suspicion. He remained there to guard the entrance to the palace while Patrick, Lord Ruthven proceeded with a hand-picked detachment to the queen's chamber. Ruthven, a cruel religious bigot, was just the man for the cowardly act they had in mind, and although for some months he had been confined to bed with a serious illness and was scarcely able to walk, he willingly volunteered for the job. He wore a helmet, and his loose robe concealed a complete suit of armour.

Mary sat down to supper as usual at 7 p.m., accompanied by her illegitimate sister, the Countess of Argyll, her brother, Lord Robert Stewart, and Rizzio. Her Master of the Household, Beaton, Erskine and one or two other servants of the privy chamber were in waiting at a side table.

At about 8 p.m., to check that the coast was clear, Darnley went up the private stairs, entered the small room where his wife was having supper and sat down familiarly beside her.

As he had expected, he found Rizzio in attendance. Once the conspirators had allowed sufficient time to elapse to be satisfied that all was in order, they followed the king up the private stairs in order to avoid any domestic servants who might have given the alarm.

Led by Ruthven and George Douglas – illegitimate son of the late Earl of Angus and illegitimate brother of Darnley's mother, Lady Lennox – as many accomplices as could crowd into the small room entered abruptly, while nearly forty more gathered in Mary's bedroom. Ruthven, his heavy armour rattling on his lank, exhausted frame, looking as grim and fearful as an animated corpse, threw himself unceremoniously into a chair. The queen indignantly demanded the meaning of this insolent intrusion, adding that he came with the appearance and in the clothing of someone who had evil in mind. Turning his hollow eyes on Rizzio, Ruthven answered that he intended evil only to the villain who stood near her. On hearing these words, Rizzio realized the danger he was in and panicked. Mary, on the other hand, as befitted one through whose veins flowed the blood of James V and his warlike ancestors, stayed calm. She turned to her husband and called on him for protection. When it became obvious that he had no intention of intervening, she ordered Ruthven to leave or be charged with treason, promising that if Rizzio was accused of any crime it would be investigated by the current parliament.

Ruthven replied only by heaping abuse on Rizzio and declaring that they were determined to take him prisoner. Rizzio, scared out of his wits, cowered in the window recess with his dagger in one hand, clasping the folds of Mary's gown with the other. Despite many threats, he remained standing behind her, shouting '*Giustizia! Giustizia!*' The assassins told Darnley to grab his wife and move her out of the way, but at this point the Master of the Household and three or four servants of the privy chamber tried to bundle Ruthven out of the room, and when his followers rushed to defend him they overturned the supper table, threw down the dishes and the candles, and announced with hideous oaths that they were going to murder Rizzio. Their rashness was nearly their undoing – if the Countess of Argyll had failed to catch one of the candles as it was falling, the room would have been plunged into darkness and their victim might have escaped.

Although swords and daggers had been drawn and pistols had been aimed at Rizzio and the queen, no blow was landed until George Douglas, seizing the dirk that Darnley wore at his side, stabbed Rizzio over Mary's shoulder. At first she had no idea what had happened, but then the unhappy Italian was dragged out into the bedroom and through the presence chamber, where the conspirators quickly finished him off, leaving his body in a pool of blood with no fewer than fifty-six wounds. Not long afterwards, they threw his body down the stairs and carried it to the porter's lodge with the king's dagger still sticking in its side. He was buried un-ceremoniously the next day but was subsequently given a more honourable burial near the Royal Vault in Holyrood Chapel. One account maintains that John Daniot, a French priest reputed to be a magician, had told Rizzio: 'Beware of a bastard.' Rizzio, thinking he referred to Moray, answered that no bastard would have much power in Scotland as long as he lived. The prophecy seemingly came true – the bastard Douglas was the first to stab him.

Once Morton, who was still guarding the gates, was informed that Rizzio had been killed as planned and that Mary was in Ruthven and Darnley's custody, he tried to seize several of the nobles lodging in the palace – the Earls of Huntly, Bothwell and Atholl, the Lords Fleming and Livingston, and Sir James Balfour – who he knew were opposed to his plan to restore the banished lords. He was unsuccessful, and several escaped, and before long the Provost of Edinburgh was alerted and the alarm was raised. The civic authorities and five or six hundred loyal citizens hurried to Holyrood and called on the queen to show herself and assure them that she was safe. But Mary, still confined in the same room where the plot had unfolded, was not allowed to answer. She later wrote to her ambassador in France that she was 'extremely threatened by the traitors, who, in her face, declared that if she spoke to the town's people they would cut her in collops and cast her over the walls'. Instead, Darnley went to the window and informed the crowd that he and the queen were well and did not need their assistance. Morton and Ruthven told them no harm had been done and begged them to return home, which they finally did.

A scene of mutual recrimination now took place between Mary and her husband, which was prolonged by the boorish behaviour of Ruthven. Returning to the queen's apartment with his hands stained with Rizzio's blood, he called for a cup of wine and, having seated himself, drained it to the dregs while Mary stood beside him. Having recovered a little from the terror that she had felt when she witnessed Rizzio being dragged away by the assassins, she rebuked Ruthven for his discourteous conduct, but he only added the use of insulting language to the crimes that he had already committed. He and the other conspirators knew, however, that Mary was seven months pregnant, and in her condition the horrific scenes had taken their toll, so he proposed to the king that they should retire, taking care to station a sufficiently strong guard at the door of Mary's chamber.

Next morning, although it was Sunday, the conspirators issued a proclamation in the king's name, without asking the queen's leave, proroguing the parliament and commanding all the lords who had come to attend it to leave Edinburgh. Illegal as it was, this proclamation was obeyed, for Morton and his accomplices had seized power, and Mary's more faithful subjects were taken so much by surprise that they were unable to offer any immediate resistance.

Although Mary was still kept in strict confinement, she did manage one attempt to escape. Sir James Melville was allowed to leave the palace early on the Sunday morning, and as he walked to the outer gate, Mary begged him for help. He approached her and asked what he could do. She told him to alert the Provost of Edinburgh. When some of the guards challenged Sir James, he told them he was just on his way to St Giles's Kirk, and they let him go. He went straight to the provost and delivered his message, but the provost protested he didn't know what to do – he had received contrary orders from the king and, besides, the people were unlikely to take up arms to revenge Rizzio's death. Later that day, Mary learned that Rizzio had been murdered, and she shed tears at the death of her faithful servant.

Between 7 and 8 p.m. the Earls of Moray and Rothes arrived from England with the other banished lords. Morton and his accomplices now found themselves in a dilemma. They had succeeded in all their immediate aims – bringing home their rebel friends, proroguing parliament, conferring on Darnley all the power he wished, murdering Rizzio and chasing from court the nobles who had formed part of the administration along with him – but only by threatening the life of their lawful sovereign, turning her own palace into a prison and becoming her gaolers. What were they to do with the queen? If they set her free, would she calmly forget what they had done or quietly submit to the new state of affairs they had established? On the other hand, did they have any grounds for ill-treating her further? Would the country allow a sovereign whose reign had hitherto been so prosperous to be deprived of her crown and her authority?

Even Darnley, always vacillating and always contemptible, was beginning to think he had gone too far. Influenced by a returning glimmer of affection for his beautiful consort, who in a month or two would bear his child, he insisted that enough was enough, as long as Mary promised to receive into favour the lords who had returned from banishment and to pardon all who had taken part in the assassination. Morton, Ruthven, Moray and the rest were extremely unwilling to consent to such a risky arrangement, but Darnley overruled their objections. On the Monday evening, articles were drawn up promising their security, and he promised to get the queen to sign them. Trusting his word, all the conspirators, including the lords who had just returned, went to supper at the Earl of Morton's with their retainers.

As soon as Mary found herself alone with Darnley she used the force of her superior mind to muster every argument to convince him how foolish he had been to associate himself with the conspirators. She didn't realize the full extent of his involvement in the plot – he had assured her that he was not to blame for Rizzio's murder, and she believed him. Eventually, she convinced him that his best hopes for advancement lay with her, not men who, having first betrayed their lawful queen, promised him a degree of power that was not theirs to bestow. Once she revealed that Huntly, Bothwell, Atholl and others had already sided with her, he agreed that they should make their escape together immediately. At midnight, accompanied only by the captain of the guard and two others, they left the palace and rode to Dunbar without stopping.

A few days later, Mary had been joined by more than half her nobles and found herself at the head of a powerful army. The conspirators, betrayed by Darnley and with next to no public support, were unable to offer much resistance. To diminish what little strength they had, Mary made a distinction between the old and the new rebels, and surprised Morton by pardoning Moray, Argyll and others, who immediately joined her and were received into favour. After staying in Dunbar for only five days, she marched back in triumph to Edinburgh. The conspirators fled in all directions to avoid the punishment they so justly deserved, Morton, Maitland, Ruthven and Lindsay heading for Newcastle.

The whole state of affairs had been transformed. Mary, who for some days had suffered so much, was once more Queen of Scots. It was not in her nature to be cruel, and her resentments never lasted long. Only two people were executed for their part in Rizzio's murder, and these were minor players. Before the end of the year, most of the principal conspirators were allowed to return to court. Ruthven died of his long-term illness a month or two after he had fled to Newcastle. Few mourned his passing, and history remembers him merely as a titled murderer.

CHAPTER IV

*B*IRTH AND ESTRANGEMENT

Although Mary had been restored to power, she was far from happy, and the recent series of treacherous upheavals had left her badly shaken. In a letter to one of her female relations in France, she wrote: 'It will grieve you to hear how entirely, in a very short time, I have changed my character, from that of the most easily satisfied and care-chasing of mortals, to one embroiled in constant turmoils and perplexities.' Mary could have borne the treachery of her nobles, but her husband's disloyalty was a severe blow. Anxious to believe his insistence that he had not been an accomplice in Rizzio's murder, she was glad when he issued a proclamation declaring that he was neither 'a partaker in, nor privy to, David's slaughter', but she could not hide from the truth for long. Randolph wrote to Cecil on 4 April 1566: 'The Queen hath seen all the covenants and bands that passed between the King and the Lords, and now findeth that his declaration before her and Council, of his innocency of the death of David, was false; and is grievously offended, that by their means he should seek to come to the crown-matrimonial.'

The young and graceful Darnley who had courted Mary was a very different person from the headstrong and unscrupulous king who had consorted with the rebels, assassinated her faithful servant and tried to steal her crown. But Mary felt more sorrow than anger at his transformation, and although she shed many a bitter tear over his betrayal of her, she still continued to love him.

The queen was now nearing the end of her pregnancy. After a short excursion to Stirling and the surrounding area, she returned to Edinburgh accompanied by Darnley, Moray, Bothwell and others. On the advice of her Privy Council, for security reasons she took up residence in Stirling Castle until she could present the country with an heir to the throne.

During April and May she lived there very quietly, amusing herself with her work and her books, and taking occasional strolls. She tried to heal the rifts among her nobles, but it was not easy to persuade her two most faithful ministers – her Chancellor, the Earl of Huntly, and her Lord High Admiral, Bothwell – to accept the return to favour of their old enemy, the Earl of Moray. It was especially galling to them that Moray and Argyll were the only persons apart from the king who were allowed to live in the castle with Mary, but she insisted on having her husband and brothers beside her during the final stages of her confinement. Huntly and Bothwell went so far as to inform her that Moray had entered into a new conspiracy with Morton and that they probably intended to take her and her child into custody as soon as it was born. Surrounded as she was by traitors, Mary found it difficult to judge the truth of this claim, and her returning affection for Moray overcame any doubts she might have had.

Meanwhile, Elizabeth was observing the situation with great interest. She was pleased at Moray's restoration to favour, and she secretly offered Morton and his friends support and protection. With her usual duplicity, she sent Henry Killigrew to Edinburgh to congratulate Mary on her recent escape and to assure her that she would have Morton expelled from England. She also recalled Randolph, whom Mary had accused of sedition. However, in return she commanded Killigrew to ask why Ruxby, a rebel and a papist, had been harboured in Scotland.

Elizabeth would have been well advised not to raise this issue. Although Ruxby pretended to be a religious refugee from England, in reality Elizabeth and her Secretary, Cecil, had sent him to Scotland on a mission to find out whether Mary was secretly corresponding with the English Catholics. He was to pretend that he was a zealous supporter of her right and title to the English crown and that he had some influence with the English Catholics, claiming they all shared his views. Once he had ingratiated himself with Mary, he was to notify Cecil of any discoveries he might make. The scheme was ingenious. Presenting himself as an avowed enemy to Elizabeth, with credentials to that effect supplied by Elizabeth herself, for some time no one suspected his real designs. However, it is unlikely he discovered anything to give Elizabeth reasonable grounds for offence since the contents of several communications in cipher between him and Cecil were never made public.

However, shortly before Killigrew's arrival, Ruxby was discovered to be a spy, and when the English ambassador tried to maintain his cover by requesting that Mary cease giving him asylum, she immediately ordered Ruxby's arrest and the seizure and examination of all his writings and ciphers. They revealed conclusive evidence of Elizabeth's cunning plot, but Mary did not react openly, and Ruxby's fate is unknown.

Early in June, realizing that she would soon give birth, Mary ordered her principal lords to attend her. She then drew up her will and sent one copy to France, placed a second in the charge of her Privy Council and kept the third herself. The day before her delivery she drafted a letter to Elizabeth announcing the event but leaving a blank space for details of the child's sex to be entered later.

Between 9 and 10 a.m. on Wednesday 19 June 1566, Mary gave birth to a son and heir. In Edinburgh, several days of celebrations began, with all the town's nobility and most of its citizens going in solemn procession to the High Church to offer thanks for the birth of a prince, and throughout Scotland the news was greeted with sincere demonstrations of joy.

The new prince's birth aroused far less satisfaction in England. Four days later, when Sir James Melville arrived in London on horseback, he found Elizabeth in good spirits at Greenwich, dancing after supper. However, the merriment came to an abrupt halt once Cecil whispered the news in her ear. She sat down with her hand on her cheek and lamented to her ladies that the Queen of Scots had given birth to a son while she herself was barren.

When Elizabeth held a formal audience with Melville the next morning, her attempts to hide her true feelings only made them more obvious. She told him gravely that the joyful news had helped her recover from a sickness that had afflicted her for fifteen days. Elizabeth agreed to be a godparent to the prince, and in response to an invitation to visit her sister to share in the happy event, she smiled and said that she wished her estate and affairs might permit it and promised to send lords and ladies to attend her.

As soon as she was well enough to leave Edinburgh Castle, Mary decided to take a holiday from the troubles of government. Her infant son was placed in the care of the Earl and Lady Mar, as governor and governess. It was a little early to make arrangements for his education, but the General Assembly had already sent a deputation to the queen to ask her to allow him to be brought up in the Reformed religion. Mary avoided giving any definite answer but took her son from his nurse and placed him in the arms of some of the churchmen. After a prayer was said over him, he gave an inarticulate murmur, which the delighted Presbyterians interpreted as 'Amen'.

As yet too frail for a long journey by horse, Mary boarded a vessel at Newhaven and sailed up the Forth to the seat of the Earl of Mar at Alloa, accompanied by Moray and other nobles. Darnley travelled to Alloa by land and stayed with Mary for most of her visit, but he was in a foul mood. The lack of deference shown him by Mary's ministers made him uneasy and he complained about their attitude continually, but his unpopularity was understandable in the circumstances. He and Moray had hated each other for a long time, he had offended Huntly and Bothwell by plotting against them with Morton, and his subsequent desertion of Morton and his faction had lost him the only friends he had. Mary was deeply upset and tried to build bridges between him and her ministers, but there were limits to what she could do. Even if she had wanted to, she could not have dismissed those ministers he considered obnoxious, since such an unconstitutional measure might have led to a second rebellion. She simply hoped that if she treated her husband kindly and attentively, others would understand that she expected them to show him equal respect.

After spending some days together at Alloa, Mary and Darnley went hunting in Peeblesshire. Finding little sport, they returned to Edinburgh on 20 August to collect the young prince, then took up residence in Stirling Castle.

A number of historians have claimed that Mary and the Earl of Bothwell were secret lovers at this time and even that Mary had fallen in love with him before she gave birth, but there is little or no evidence for this. It is true that shortly after the assassination of Rizzio (who some authorities also suggest was her lover), Bothwell was loaded with favours and preferment, but it was quite understandable for Mary to confer some reward on a nobleman whose power and loyalty were the chief means of preserving her on a tottering throne. Bothwell certainly wielded great influence at court, but there is no evidence that he was as influential as Moray or more so than Huntly. Furthermore, he had only just married the young, elegant Lady Jane Gordon, the sister of his friend the Earl of Huntly, about three months previously, and was currently far away from Mary in some of the southern shires, attending to his duties as Lieutenant of the Borders.

Having spent some time with Darnley at Stirling, Mary returned to Edinburgh to attend to public business on 11 or 12

September. She wanted Darnley to accompany her, but he refused to travel in the company of her ministers. On 21 September she returned to Stirling, but on 23 September her Privy Council recalled her to Edinburgh. She left the wayward Darnley in the company of the French ambassador, Le Croc, hoping that his wisdom and experience might be of benefit to him.

Mary had been in Edinburgh for only a few days when on 29 September she received a worrying letter from the Earl of Lennox, Darnley's father, who had visited his son in Stirling. Darnley had told him that he intended to leave the country and proceed to the Continent. Both Lennox and Le Croc had done all they could to dissuade him, but he seemed determined. Mary immediately laid her father-in-law's letter before her Privy Council, which resolved to talk to Darnley to establish his reasons so that they could advise Mary what to do. That evening, Darnley arrived at Holyrood, but when he was informed that Argyll, Moray and Rothes were with the queen, he declared he would not enter the palace until they left. Mary, glad to see him, took this petulant behaviour as mildly as possible, left the palace to meet her husband and led him to her own apartment where they spent the night together.

Next day, Mary persuaded Darnley to attend a meeting of her Privy Council. They asked him whether he had decided to leave the country and, if so, why. They added that if he had any complaint against any subjects of the realm, of whatever station, immediate action would be taken to resolve the matter. Mary took him by the hand and begged him affectionately to tell her if she had given him any reason to leave.

Although she had a clear conscience, she understood she might have offended him unintentionally, and she was willing to make amends. Darnley answered that he found no fault in the queen, but he peevishly refused to discuss the matter further. Taking his leave, he said to Mary: 'Farewell, Madam. You shall not see my face for a long while.' He said goodbye to Le Croc and then, turning coldly to the Lords of the Council, said: 'Gentlemen, adieu.'

Shortly afterwards, Mary received a letter from Darnley in which he raised two complaints: first, that Mary no longer entrusted to him such authority nor took such pains to advance him and make him honoured in the nation as she had at first; and second, that he had no attendants and the nobility avoided his company. Mary replied that if this was the case, he should blame himself, not her. She had come to regret bestowing so many honours on him initially, since they had served as a cloak for conspiracy. However, despite the fact that Rizzio's murderers had entered her chamber with Darnley's assistance and had named him as chief conspirator, she had never accused him and was willing to take his word. His lack of attendants was his own fault, since she had always offered him her own servants. As for the nobility, he had made no efforts to win them over, even forbidding the noblemen she had appointed to attend him to enter his room. If the lords had abandoned him, his own behaviour towards them was to blame. Unless he tried to win their respect, she would find it difficult to persuade them to agree to allow him to play a part in government.

The southern marches of Scotland were now in near continuous upheaval, and the insurrections of Moray and Morton, both aided by Elizabeth, had incited the Borderers to actions that cried out for legal measures. Mary had intended to hold assizes in Liddisdale in August, but since it was harvest time, she postponed leaving Edinburgh until October. On 6 or 7 October, she sent Bothwell, her lieutenant, to make the necessary preparations for her arrival, and on 8 October the queen and her court set out, the noblemen and gentlemen of the southern shires having been summoned to meet her with their retainers at Melrose.

On 10 October she arrived at Jedburgh. She had received news that on the very day she left Edinburgh, Bothwell had been attacked and badly wounded by some unruly Borderers soon after reaching Hermitage Castle, about eighteen miles from Jedburgh. A number of reasons have been given for the attack on Bothwell. Some say that it was an act of revenge by Morton, who had bribed the Elliot clan. Others claim that his assailants were simply common thieves. But whatever the reasons, by the time the report reached Mary, as usual the account had been exaggerated. Her duties at Jedburgh prevented her from establishing the facts for several days, but finding herself free on 18 October, she rode to Hermitage with some attendants, both to find out how he was and to learn to what extent her authority had been flouted by the attack on him. She stayed only an hour or two, then returned to Jedburgh the same evening.

On 17 October Mary fell dangerously ill with a severe fever, and there were fears for her life for ten days – indeed, at one point Edinburgh received reports that she was dead. The fever was accompanied by fainting fits that frequently lasted three or four hours, during which she was to all appearances lifeless, her body motionless, her eyes closed, her mouth clamped shut, and her feet and arms stiff and cold. On regaining consciousness she suffered the most dreadful pain, her limbs drawn writhingly together.

Her illness lasted so long that she began to doubt she would ever recover. She summoned the noblemen who were with her, in particular Moray, Huntly, Rothes and Bothwell, and gave them what she believed to be her dying advice and instructions. After requesting her Privy Council to pray for her and professing her willingness to submit to the will of heaven, Mary placed her son in their care. She begged them to give every attention to his education, allowing no one near him whose example might corrupt his manners or his mind, and to bring him up to be virtuous and godly. She strongly advised them to continue to show the same tolerance in religious matters that she had practised, and she concluded by asking that suitable provision should be made for the servants of her household, to whom Mary was scrupulously attentive, and who all loved her very much. Fortunately, however, her illness abated, and her youth and strong constitution meant she was soon on the mend.

Darnley, who was with his father in Glasgow, did not hear of the queen's illness until a day or two after it began, and as soon as he learned how serious it was he decided to visit her. This again shows the contrast between his attitude to Mary and his extreme dislike of her ministers. He had no quarrel with Mary, although his love for her was not as strong and pure as it should have been and was easily forgotten when it stood in the way of his own selfish wishes, and he tried hard to remain on friendly terms with her. When he had left her at Holyrood he had said that she wouldn't see him for a long while, but her unexpected illness prompted him to change his mind.

By the time he arrived on 28 October, Mary was better, but since she was still convalescing, Darnley's arrival was far from welcome to her ministers. If Mary died, one of them would be appointed regent – an office to which they knew that Darnley, as father of the young prince, had strong claims. It was in their interests, therefore, to try to drive a wedge between the queen and her husband, as they were afraid that the affection between them might be rekindled. When Mary was cool and dispassionate, they knew they could manage her easily, but when she was in love, Mary always had her own way. They gave Darnley such a forbidding reception that, having spent a day and a night with Mary, he was glad to leave.

On 9 November the queen and her court left Jedburgh and went to Kelso, where she stayed for two days before proceeding to Berwick, attended by eight hundred knights and gentlemen on horseback. From Berwick she rode to Dunbar, and from Dunbar via Tantallon to Craigmillar, where she arrived on 20 November.

In December, during Mary's three-week stay at Craigmillar, her Privy Council made a startling proposal. Its originator was the Earl of Bothwell, who was now an active cabinet minister and officer of state since Moray and Darnley, the only people Mary had been willing to allow a major role in government, had deceived her, and she had no idea who else to appoint as an adviser.

Mary tried hard to be even-handed in her treatment of

her ministers, Moray, Bothwell, Maitland, Argyll (the Justice General) and Huntly (the Chancellor). Rizzio had been faithful to her, and she had listened to him with some deference, but even if he had lived, he could never have served as Prime Minister. The Earl of Morton would certainly have wanted the job, but he had unwisely chosen to oppose the queen in favour of Darnley. As a result, Morton had been banished and Moray reinstated, but although she was still fond of her brother, Mary could no longer trust him fully. Gratitude and common justice meant she could not elevate him above those who had supported her and remained loyal through the recent troubles, particularly Huntly and Bothwell.

Bothwell's rank and services undoubtedly made him a strong contender for the post of Prime Minister, but Mary had never liked him. He had conducted himself better since being reinstated after his banishment, but experience had taught Mary not to trust appearances, so although Bothwell had more influence than before, she did not allow him to play a major role in her councils. After Rizzio's murder, part of Maitland's lands had been given to Bothwell. She had later restored Maitland to his lands and place at court in direct opposition to Bothwell's wishes, and this had led to harsh words between him and Moray in the queen's presence. Nevertheless, Bothwell began to believe that if he could only be patient, power was within his grasp. With this in mind, at the beginning of October he prevailed on Moray, Huntly and Argyll to join with him in a bond of mutual friendship and support. He set aside any enmity he may have felt towards Morton and let him know that he would petition the queen for his recall, and – his boldest move yet – he canvassed the rest of the Privy Council about the propriety of suggesting to Mary that she divorce her husband.

Although Darnley had fallen from grace, he stood directly in the path of Bothwell's ambition. He had to be disposed of, and since violence could only be the last resort, seeking a divorce was the best course of action. He knew that the nobility would not object – for some time they had been trying to persuade the nation at large, and Mary in particular, that it was Darnley's conduct that made her unhappy and was the source of most of the troubles. There was some truth in this view, but although the ministers preferred not to acknowledge it, it was their role in government and the fact that Mary needed their assistance that was largely responsible for the rift between her and Darnley.

By agreeing to help seek Morton's pardon and making other promises, Bothwell persuaded Moray, Huntly, Argyll and Maitland of Lethington to join him in advising the queen to agree to a divorce. This would require the consent of the pope, and Moray at first expressed some religious scruples, but these were soon overcome. The lords held an audience with the queen, and Lethington, who had a better command of words than the rest, began by reminding her of the offences that Darnley had committed, adding that if Darnley remained with her, he would betray her again. He then proposed the divorce, promising that he and the other lords would obtain the consent of parliament on condition that she agreed to pardon Morton, Ruthven, Lindsay and their friends, whose aid would be necessary to secure a majority.

69

But Lethington and the rest soon found that they had misjudged Mary's real feelings towards her husband. At first she would not agree even to talk about the subject at all, and only after much cajoling did she state two objections that she regarded as insuperable: in the first place she did not understand how the divorce could be carried out lawfully, and, secondly, it would harm her son and she would never allow that. Bothwell tried to persuade her by arguing that although his father and mother would be divorced, there would never be any doubt about his succession to his paternal estates, but Mary answered firmly: 'I will that you do nothing by which any spot may be laid on my honour and conscience; and therefore, I pray ye rather let the matter be in the estate as it is, abiding till God of His goodness put a remedy to it. That you believe would do me service, may possibly turn to my hurt and displeasure.' As for Darnley, she hoped he would soon change for the better. Finally, prompted by the desire to escape her many cares, she said she would perhaps go to France for a while and stay there until her husband saw the error of his ways. She then dismissed Bothwell and his friends, who retired to dream up new schemes.

On 11 December Mary went to Stirling to make arrangements for the baptism of her son, which she was determined to celebrate with the pomp and magnificence his future prospects justified. Darnley had travelled to Stirling two days earlier, having stayed with the queen at Craigmillar Castle for a week before returning to Edinburgh with her. Ambassadors had arrived from England, France, Piedmont and Savoy to be present at the ceremony. The pope had also proposed sending a nuncio to Scotland, but Mary had had the good sense to know that such an act would greatly offend her more bigoted subjects. She might also have feared that his presence could have allowed secret negotiations for the proposed divorce to take place.

The splendour of Mary's preparations for the baptism astonished the sober-minded Presbyterians, Knox protesting: 'The excessive expenses and superfluous apparel, which were prepared at that time, exceeded far all the preparations that ever had been devised or set forth before in this country.' To meet the extraordinary cost of entertaining so many ambassadors, the queen was permitted to levy a tax of £12,000: £6,000 from the spiritual estate, £4,000 from the barons and freeholders, and £2,000 from the boroughs. Elizabeth, as if sharing in Mary's maternal feelings, sent her ambassador, the Earl of Bedford, to Stirling with a gorgeous train and a present of a golden font valued at more than £1,000. She instructed Bedford to say jocularly that it had been made as soon as she had heard of the prince's birth, and that it was large enough then, but since the prince had probably outgrown it by now it might be kept for the next child. It was too late in the season for Elizabeth to send any of the ladies of her realm to Scotland so she appointed the Countess of Argyll to represent her as godmother because she understood that Mary held her in great esteem.

In the days leading up to the ceremony, Mary held splendid banquets for the ambassadors and their entourages during which there was evidence of some jealousy between the English and French envoys regarding matters of precedence. Mary was inclined to favour the English, having closer connections with England than France nowadays, but the tensions were never far beneath the surface. For one banquet, one of Mary's French servants, Sebastian, had built a great table that contained an ingenious mechanism. When the doors of the great hall where the feast was being held were thrown open, it moved in, apparently of its own accord, covered with delicacies of all sorts. A band of musicians, clothed like maidens, singing and accompanying themselves on various instruments, surrounded the pageant. However, it was preceded – and this was the cause of the offence – by a number of men dressed like satyrs, with long tails, carrying whips in their hands. These satyrs were not content to ride round the table but put their hands behind their backs and wagged their tails in the faces of the Englishmen, who took grave offence and thought they were being mocked. A member of the Earl of Bedford's party told Melville that if the queen had not been present, 'he would put a dagger to the heart of the French knave Sebastian, whom he alleged did it for despite that the Queen made more of them than of the Frenchmen'. The queen and Bedford, who understood it was just a joke, had some difficulty calming down the hotheaded southerners.

However, more serious matters claimed Mary's attention during this period. When she arrived at Stirling, she found that Darnley had chosen not to stay at the castle but was lodging in a private house. When she arrived he joined her in the castle, but his attitude towards Mary's ministers was unchanged, and the feeling was mutual. Mary was anxious to avoid any embarrassing incidents in front of the foreign ambassadors, but Darnley was as stubborn as ever. Although he had given up thoughts of going abroad, it was only because he was hatching a new plot at home. Surrounded by gaiety, he remained sullen and discontented, shutting himself up in his own apartment and associating with no one except his wife and the French envoy, Le Croc. His mood was not improved by the fact that Elizabeth had reputedly forbidden Bedford or any of his retinue to give him the title 'King' – she was still angry that he had defied her will by marrying – and this probably contributed to his refusal to attend the christening of his son.

Mary had another problem: the baptism was to be a Catholic ritual, so most of her lords not only refused to take any part in the ceremony but even to attend it. Mary tried to persuade Moray, Huntly and Bothwell, but in vain – they were unwilling to risk alienating the Reformers.

Between 5 and 6 p.m. on 19 December 1566, the baptism for which so many preparations had been made took place. The Earls of Atholl and Eglinton and the Lords Semple and Ross, being of the Catholic persuasion, carried the instruments. The Archbishop of St Andrews, assisted by the Bishops of Dunblane, Dunkeld and Ross, received the prince at the door of the chapel. The Countess of Argyll held the infant at the font, and the archbishop baptised him Charles James, James Charles, Prince and Steward of Scotland, Duke of Rothesay, Earl of Carrick, Lord of the Isles and Baron of Renfrew. These names and titles were proclaimed three times by heralds to the sound of trumpets. Mary called her son Charles after the King of France, her brother-in-law, but she also gave him the name James because her father and all the good kings of Scotland had been called by that name. Throughout the ceremony, the Scottish Protestant nobles and the Earl of Bedford remained at the door of the chapel, and the Countess of Argyll later had to do penance for the part she played in the proceedings.

Elizabeth was right in supposing that the infant James had outgrown her font. He was a remarkably stout and healthy child, and his godparents' arms ached from holding him. Mary was very proud of her son, and from his earliest infancy he was given a most princely upbringing, looking after him creating quite a number of jobs. Lady Mar continued as his governess. Mistress Margaret Little, his head nurse, had four or five women under her with titles such as 'Keepers of the King's Clothes', and five ladies of distinction were appointed to the honourable office of 'Rockers of the Prince's Cradle'. Even at this early age James had a master cook, a foreman and three other servitors, plus one for his pantry, one for his wine and two for his ale cellar. He had three 'chalmer-chields', one 'furnisher of coals' and one pastry cook or confectioner. Five musicians (or 'violars') completed his staff. To fill so many mouths there was a fixed allowance of provisions, consisting of bread, beef, veal, mutton, capons, chickens, pigeons, fish, pottages, wine and ale.

Mary's grace and affability at the baptism won universal admiration, and the most favourable impressions the ambassadors took home with them were enhanced by the valuable gifts she gave them. But all the time she was making an effort to keep up appearances and put on a brave face, and on one occasion Le Croc found her lying on her bed, weeping inconsolably. Mary had good reason to weep: her ministers were determined to force her to pardon the Earl of Morton and seventy-five of his accomplices. One of Mary's failings was the ease with which she could be persuaded to forgive the worst transgressions, and Moray had prevailed on Cecil to induce Elizabeth to ask Bedford to add his influence to that of Mary's Privy Council on behalf of Morton. The queen could not resist such a united front, and all the conspirators against Rizzio were pardoned except George Douglas, who had grabbed the king's dagger and been the first to stab Rizzio, and Andrew Kerr, who had threatened to shoot the queen during the affray.

Darnley was naturally livid that any of his former accomplices had been rehabilitated. Their return to favour would make it even harder for him to secure advancement, and it coincided with a plan he was reportedly working on to seize the young prince and, after crowning him, to take over the government as his father. Whether this report was true or not (and it may have been the reason why the queen moved from Stirling to Edinburgh shortly afterwards), it is certain that Darnley could not bear to be in the company of some of the noblemen attending court and that either he or they would have to leave. He left Stirling on 24 December – the very day on which Morton's pardon was signed – to visit his father at Glasgow. His quarrel had not been with Mary, with whom he had been living for the last ten days, and he intended rejoining her in Edinburgh as soon as she had paid some Christmas visits in the Stirling area.

CHAPTER

V

DEATH OF A KING

Bothwell had decided the time was ripe to put his scheme into action. He was in league with the scarcely less ambitious Moray, using his name and authority to strengthen his own influence, but only told him as much of his plans as he thought advisable.

It appears that Bothwell was the only Scottish baron of this period over whom Moray never had any control – indeed, his character was not one that would have brooked control. Banished after his conspiracy with Huntly and others to remove Moray failed, Bothwell had not been recalled until Moray had fallen into disgrace, and although he had been pardoned, he had never fully regained Mary's favour. Now he aimed to become not merely Prime Minister, but king.

Having decided that since Mary would not divorce Darnley, Darnley would have to die, Bothwell began to consider what to do afterwards. He could never legally marry Mary as long as his own marriage to Lady Jane Gordon lasted, so he would have to divorce her. There would be no time to go through the normal legal channels, so, hiding his real motives, he used his influence with the queen to reinstate the ancient jurisdiction of the Catholic Consistorial Courts, which had been abolished by the Reformed Parliament of 1560, when the ordinary civil Commissary Courts were established in their place. Mary abolished the Commissary Courts and restored the Archbishop of St Andrews, the Primate of Scotland, to the ancient Consistorial Jurisdiction under canon law. Not only did this win Bothwell the friendship of the primate, it established a court where the Catholic plea of consanguinity could be advanced – the only plausible pretext for annulling his marriage.

The Reformers understandably took great offence at Mary's action, and when the primate came to Edinburgh at the beginning of January to hold his court, Moray took Mary to task. Bothwell's attempts to defend the decision were unsuccessful, and Mary was forced to suspend the primate's court proceedings.

Meanwhile, Darnley had fallen ill. Some believe he had been poisoned by one of Bothwell's cronies, but he was almost certainly suffering from smallpox, which was widespread in Glasgow at the time. On 13 January 1567, Mary returned from Stirling to Edinburgh and installed her son in Holyrood House. As soon as she heard of Darnley's illness she sent her own physician to attend him, and when his condition became serious, she immediately set out to visit him.

On arriving at Glasgow, Mary found her husband convalescing but still very weak. She lodged in the same house as him, but since his disease was considered infectious, they had separate apartments. Finding that his recent approach to the brink of the grave had improved his disposition, and hoping to regain his confidence by nursing him during his recovery, she gladly agreed when he suggested she take him back with her to Edinburgh or its vicinity. She suggested that Craigmillar Castle would be better suited to convalescence, but for some reason he objected, so she wrote to Secretary Maitland to procure accommodation for her husband in Edinburgh. Darnley disliked the Lords of the Privy Council too much to contemplate staying at Holyrood, and besides, the physicians thought the young prince might catch the infection from the servants who would attend them both.

When Mary wrote to Maitland, she had no idea she was addressing an accomplice in the plot to murder her husband. Maitland showed her letter to Bothwell, and they decided to recommend that Darnley stay at Provost Robert Balfour's house of Kirk o' Field, on what is now Drummond Street, on the grounds that its airy location would help his recovery, although the real reason was that it stood by itself in a comparatively solitary part of the town.

On Monday 17 January Mary and Darnley left Glasgow and travelled in stages via Callander and Linlithgow, arriving in Edinburgh on the Thursday. Mary spent a great deal of time with Darnley during the ten days he spent in his new residence, and on several nights slept in the room below her husband's rather than returning to Holyrood Palace at a late hour. Darnley was still very much an invalid and needed constant attention. Following Mary's example, some of the nobles were prepared to forget their former disagreements with Darnley and visited him occasionally. After sitting for hours in her husband's sickroom, Mary sometimes took the air in the neighbouring gardens of the Dominican convent and sometimes brought her band of musicians from Holyrood to perform for her and Darnley. Everything was going so smoothly that neither the victim nor his friends had any suspicion of what was about to happen.

Bothwell had taken advantage of Mary's visit to Glasgow to travel secretly with Maitland and a notorious relation of Morton's, Archibald Douglas, to Whittingham, near Dunbar, to meet Morton and obtain his consent to Darnley's murder. Morton, who had only recently returned from England, had no wish to prevent the murder, but before he would agree to play an active part he insisted on written proof of Bothwell's audacious claim that Mary approved of it. Although Bothwell could not provide this, Morton had no objections to playing a passive role in the conspiracy. Bothwell, Maitland and Douglas returned to Edinburgh, and Morton proceeded to St Andrews, on the understanding that Bothwell was to keep him informed of the plot's progress.

Soon afterwards, Lord Robert Stewart, Moray's brother, informed Darnley that there was a plot to murder him in three days' time. Darnley immediately told Mary, who sent for Stewart and questioned him in the presence of her husband and Moray. Afraid of placing himself in danger, Stewart denied he had ever told Darnley any such thing. An argument ensued, and even if Moray had known nothing of Bothwell's scheme earlier, his suspicions must have been aroused by now. Realizing that he had better make himself scarce, he claimed that his wife was ill and left Edinburgh to attend her.

A number of nobles had no doubt been persuaded either to assist Bothwell or to remain quiet about the plot. One of his accomplices declared later that Bothwell had shown him a bond signed by Huntly, Argyll, Maitland and Sir James

Balfour which read: 'That for as much as it was thought expedient and most profitable for the commonwealth, by the whole nobility and Lords under subscribed, that such a young fool and proud tyrant should not reign, nor bear rule over them, for diverse causes, therefore, these all had concluded, that he should be put off by one way or other, and whosoever should take the deed in hand, or do it, they should defend and fortify it as themselves, for it should be every one of their own, reckoned and holden done by themselves.' Bothwell claimed to another of his accomplices that Argyll, Huntly, Morton, Maitland, Ruthven and Lindsay had promised their support, and when asked what part Moray would play, he answered: 'He does not wish to intermeddle with it; he does not mean either to aid or hinder us.'

Whoever his co-conspirators were, it was Bothwell whose lawless ambition hatched the plan and whose hand was to strike the decisive blow. Everything was now arranged. His retainers were gathered round him, four or five of the country's most powerful ministers knew of his plot and did not disapprove of it, he had many friends at court who would support him either for political or personal motives, and Darnley and the queen were unsuspecting and unprotected. The crown was almost within his grasp.

Bothwell had recruited eight men to carry out the murder, four of whom were servants – Dalgleish, Wilson, Powrie and Nicolas Haubert, alias 'French Paris'. Haubert, a Frenchman, had been Bothwell's servant for a long time, but on his master's recommendation he was taken into the queen's service shortly before her husband's death, allowing Bothwell to obtain the keys to some of the doors of the Kirk o' Field house and have copies made. The other four were minor lairds who had squandered their inheritance in idleness and dissipation and were willing to take any risk to improve their fortunes – the Laird of Ormiston, his uncle, Hob Ormiston, John Hepburn of Bolton and John Hay of Tallo. Bothwell wanted Maitland, Morton and one or two others to send some of their servants to assist in the murder, but if they ever promised to do so, it appears they did not keep their word. However, Archibald Douglas was in the immediate neighbourhood with two servants when the crime took place.

Despite holding a number of secret meetings with his four principal accomplices, Bothwell had still not decided how the king was to be killed. The initial plan was to attack Darnley while he was taking one of his occasional walks in the gardens adjoining Kirk o' Field, but there were doubts that this would succeed and there was every probability that the assassins would be discovered. The next suggestion was to enter the house at midnight and stab the king as he lay in bed, but a servant usually slept in the same room, and there were always one or two in the adjoining room who might have resisted or escaped to identify the criminals later.

After much deliberation it was decided to use gunpowder – if the whole premises were blown up, any evidence would be likely to be buried in the ruins. Dunbar Castle, of which Bothwell was lord, had a supply of powder, and this was smuggled into Bothwell's Edinburgh lodgings very near Holyrood Palace. The next step was to decide on what night they could blow up the house without endangering the safety of the queen, since Bothwell had no desire for her to share her husband's fate. She frequently slept at Kirk o' Field, and it was difficult to tell in advance when she would choose to spend the night at Holyrood.

The final preparations for Darnley's assassination were made on Sunday 9 February 1567. Bothwell learned that the queen intended to attend a late-evening masque in Holyrood Palace to celebrate the marriage of her French servant, Sebastian, to Margaret Carwood, one of her ladies in waiting, so she would not be spending the night at Kirk o' Field. At dusk he assembled his accomplices and told them that the time had come for him to call on their services. Between 7 and 8 p.m. he had to attend a banquet for the queen given by the Bishop of Argyll at John Balfour's house, but they were to be ready as soon as the company broke up, when he promised to join them. The queen took supper at Holyrood before attending the banquet. She rose from the supper table at around 9 p.m., and the Earls of Argyll, Huntly and Cassilis accompanied her to visit her husband at Kirk o' Field.

Bothwell called Paris, who was waiting on the queen, aside and took him to the lodgings of the Laird of Ormiston, where they met Hay and Hepburn, and they went together down Blackfriars Wynd. They passed through a gate in the Dominican monastery wall, which ran near the foot of the wynd, and crossing the gardens, came to another wall immediately behind Darnley's house. Meanwhile, Dalgleish and Wilson divided the gunpowder into bags at Bothwell's lodgings and loaded them into trunks which they placed on horseback. There was too much for one load, so they had to make two trips to Kirk o' Field. It was unsafe for them to approach any nearer than the convent gate at the foot of Blackfriars Wynd, so Ormiston, Hepburn and Hay met them there and carried the powder up to the house. When they had finished they were ordered to return home, and as they passed up Blackfriars Wynd, Powrie, as if suddenly conscience-struck, said to Wilson: 'Jesu! Whatna a gait is this we are ganging? I trow it be not good.' Neither of them had seen Bothwell, for he kept his distance, walking up and down the Cowgate until the others had hidden the powder.

A large, empty barrel had been concealed in the convent gardens, and they intended to place all the bags inside it, carry it into the house by the lower back door and place it in the queen's bedroom, immediately under the king's. Paris, as the queen's valet-de-chambre, had the keys to the lower flat and was now in Mary's apartment ready to receive the powder, but the barrel was so large that it would not fit through the back door, so they had to carry the bags into the bedroom one by one, where they emptied them in a heap on the floor. Bothwell, still walking anxiously to and fro, was alarmed by the delay and came to ask if all was ready. He was afraid that the company upstairs, including the queen and several of her nobility and ladies in waiting, might suddenly emerge and discover them.

When everything was finally ready, they all left the lower part of the house, except Hepburn and Hay, who were locked into the room with the gunpowder to keep watch there until the others returned. Having dismissed the others, Bothwell went upstairs and joined the queen and her friends in Darnley's apartment, as if he had just arrived. Shortly afterwards, when Paris entered, the queen remembered she had to attend Sebastian's masque and took her leave of her husband at about 11 p.m.

Accompanied by Bothwell, Argyll, Huntly, Cassilis, Paris and others, Mary walked to the palace up Blackfriars' Wynd, then down the Canongate. Just as she was about to enter Holyrood House she met one of Bothwell's servants (either Dalgleish or Powrie) and asked him where he had been, since he smelt so strongly of gunpowder. He made some plausible excuse, and they continued on their way. Bothwell was anxious to avoid any suspicion and above all wanted to prevent Mary suspecting him, so he stayed near the queen.

On entering the apartment where the masque was being held, Paris, who had neither the courage nor the cunning necessary to carry him through such a villainous deed, went to stand by himself in a corner, looking miserable. Bothwell, fearing that his behaviour might attract attention, went up to him and angrily demanded why he looked so sad, telling him in a whisper that if he kept looking so down in the mouth in the queen's presence he would suffer for it. Paris answered despondently that he did not care what became of himself as long as he could have permission to go home to bed, for he was ill.

'No,' whispered Bothwell, 'you must remain with me; would you leave those two gentlemen, Hay and Hepburn, locked up where they now are?'

'Alas!' answered Paris, 'what more must I do this night? I have no heart for this business.' Bothwell put an end to the conversation by ordering Paris to follow him immediately.

At his lodgings, Bothwell exchanged his rich, courtly clothes for a white canvas doublet and wrapped himself in his riding cloak. Taking Paris, Powrie, Wilson and Dalgleish with him, he left the building, but the party was challenged by one of the sentries at the door of the queen's garden: 'Who goes there?'

'Friends.'

'What friends?'

'Friends to my Lord Bothwell.'

They proceeded up the Canongate until they came to Netherbow Port, the lower gate of the city, which was shut. They called to the porter, John Galloway, and asked him to open it. Galloway was not well pleased to be roused at so late an hour, and he kept them waiting for some time. As they entered, he asked what they were doing out of their beds at that time of night, but they gave him no answer. Once inside, they called at Ormiston's lodgings in the High Street, but finding he was not at home, went without him down a close below Blackfriars' Wynd and entered the gate to the convent gardens. They crossed to the back wall behind Darnley's residence, and Dalgleish, Wilson and Powrie were ordered to wait there while Bothwell and Paris climbed over the wall.

Entering the lower part of the house, they unlocked the door of the room in which they had left Hay and Hepburn, and the four discussed how best to set fire to the great heap of gunpowder on the floor. They took a piece of lint three or four inches long, lit one end of it and laid the other on the powder, knowing that it would burn slowly enough to give them time to retire to a safe distance. They then joined Dalgleish, Wilson and Powrie in the convent gardens and stood waiting anxiously for the explosion.

Darnley had gone to bed within an hour of the queen's departure. As usual, his servant, William Taylor, was asleep in the same room, and Thomas Nelson, Edward Simmons and a boy were sleeping in the servants' apartment on the same floor, nearer the town wall.

After a quarter of an hour the conspirators were still waiting for something to happen. Bothwell became impatient, and if the others had not stopped him and pointed out the obvious danger, he would have returned and looked through the back window of the bedroom to see whether the lint was still burning. Finally, all doubts were dispelled when an explosion, so immense that it shook the whole town and startled the inhabitants from their sleep, blew the house of Kirk o' Field into a thousand pieces, leaving scarcely a trace of its walls standing. Paris, almost senseless with fear, fell to the ground, and even Bothwell felt a momentary surge of panic.

Without waiting to assess the full extent of the damage, the conspirators hurried out of the convent gate, and once they reached Cowgate, they separated and took different routes to Netherbow Port. They were keen to avoid disturbing the porter again in case he suspected something, so they went down a close on the north side of the High Street, immediately above the city gate, hoping to be able to drop from the wall into Leith Wynd, but Bothwell, one of his hands still weak from a wound received at Hermitage Castle, found it too high. They had no option but to disturb John Galloway again, but once they told him they were friends of the Earl of Bothwell, he did not question them further. On entering the Canongate they saw some people coming up the street, so Bothwell ducked down St Mary's Wynd and went to his lodgings by the back road. The sentries at the door of the queen's garden challenged them again, and they answered that they were friends of the Earl of Bothwell carrying dispatches to him from the country. The sentinels asked whether they knew what had caused the noise they had heard a short time earlier, but they told them that they had no idea.

When Bothwell arrived home he called for a drink, took off his clothes and went to bed immediately. He had not been there more than half an hour when the news was brought to him that the house of Kirk o' Field had been blown up and the king was dead. Exclaiming that there must be treason afoot and pretending to be shocked and indignant, he rose and put on the same clothes he had worn when he was last with the queen. Huntly and others soon joined him, and after hearing from them what little was known so far, they decided to go to the palace to inform Mary of what had happened.

They found her alarmed and anxious to see them, since some vague rumours of the incident had already reached her. They broke the news to her as gradually and gently as possible, attributing Darnley's death either to the accidental explosion of some gunpowder in the neighbourhood or the effects of lightning. Mary was inconsolable, and realizing it was pointless trying to reason with her at this point, Bothwell and the other lords left her at daybreak and proceeded to Kirk o' Field.

They found everything in a state of confusion, the house in ruins and the townspeople gathered round it in dismay. Of the five people who were in the house at the time of the explosion, one only survived. Darnley and the servant who had shared his room had suffered the worst effects of the explosion. They had been thrown through the air over the town wall and across the lane on the other side, and were found lying a short distance from each other in a garden to the south of the lane, both in their night-clothes and with few external signs of injury. Simmons, Nelson and the boy, being nearer the town wall, had been more protected from the explosion but had been buried in the ruins, and only Nelson had been dug out alive. Bothwell ordered the bodies to be removed to an adjoining house and placed under guard by sentries from the palace.

Henry Stewart, Lord Darnley, Duke of Albany and King of Scotland, died at the age of twenty-one in the eighteenth month of his reign. His sudden, violent death excited a degree of compassion and interest in him that few had felt when he was alive. To Scotland he had been only a cause of civil war, to his nobility an object of contempt, pity or hatred, and to his wife a constant source of sorrow and misfortune. But for all his faults, no one in Scotland lamented him more sincerely than Mary, who had loved him deeply. She had too much good sense to believe that Darnley, as king, was a loss to the country. The tears she shed for him were not those of a queen but of a wife.

The day after her husband's death, Mary shut herself up in her own apartment and would see no one. Bothwell was anxious to talk to her, but she was overcome with grief. Confusion reigned in Edinburgh, rumours about what had really happened to Darnley were rife, and at Bothwell's instigation, most of Mary's nobles were trying to persuade her that her husband's death was either an accident or perpetrated by unknown traitors who had intended to assassinate her too.

On Tuesday 11 February, two days after the murder, she received a dispatch dated 27 January from the Archbishop of Glasgow, her ambassador in Paris, warning her that her recent pardon of Morton, Ruthven, Lindsay and others might lead to trouble. Mary replied with an account of the few facts that were known of the murder and pledged to seek out and vigorously punish her husband's murderers. A proclamation was issued the next day, immediately after an inquisition by the Justice General, offering a reward of £2,000 and 'an honest yearly rent' to anyone who would reveal 'the persons, devisers, counsellors, or actual committers of the said mischievous and treasonable murder', and promising a free pardon even if the informant had been an accomplice to the crime.

Fearing another attempt on her own life, Mary moved to the greater security of the castle and remained shut up in a dark chamber hung with black until after Darnley's burial. He lay in Holyrood Chapel from 12 to 15 February, and once his body had been embalmed, he was buried in the Royal Vault alongside King James V, his first wife, Magdalene, and his two infant sons, Mary's brothers. Religious disagreements between Mary and her nobles about the king's funeral ceremony meant that it was a quiet affair and took place at night.

Meanwhile, Bothwell kept his head down, carrying out his usual duties at court and taking care to attend all the Privy Council meetings. However, perhaps at the prompting of Moray or some of his other accomplices, suspicion fell on him, and a few days after the proclamation a placard was set up at night on the door of Edinburgh Tolbooth claiming that

89

Bothwell, James Balfour, David Chalmers and John Spence were the principal perpetrators of the crime and that the queen herself had agreed to it. Although accused herself, Mary was so keen to find the murderers that without waiting for the advice of her Privy Council she issued another proclamation asking the author of the placard to come forward and promising the reward if any of the allegations could be proved. A second placard appeared in response, demanding that the money be lodged with honest brokers, that three of the queen's servants it named be arrested and promising that as soon as these conditions were complied with the author and four witnesses would reveal themselves. Faced with such evasive demands, it was decided not to comply. Bothwell's name being mentioned in these placards in conjunction with the queen acted in his favour: knowing she was innocent, she naturally supposed that the charge against him was equally false.

In desperation, Mary tried to imagine who might have carried out the murder. Moray was living quietly in Fife. Her secretary, Maitland, was carrying on with official business as usual. Morton had not yet returned to court and was also in Fife. The Archbishop of St Andrews was busy bolstering up the last remains of Catholicism. Atholl, Caithness, Huntly, Argyll, Bothwell, Cassilis and Sutherland were attending the queen as faithful servants should. Whom should she suspect? Moray had left town suddenly on the very day of Darnley's death and had hated him from the beginning. Morton had recently returned from banishment, which had resulted from Darnley's treachery, and had assassinated Rizzio with far less provocation. Argyll had lost some of his possessions to the

Lennox family, and the king's death might help him get them back. The Hamiltons had long been enemies of the House of Lennox and Darnley had ended any hopes they might have had of succeeding to the throne. It was less likely to be Huntly, Atholl or Bothwell because they had never been in direct conflict with Darnley.

Surrounded by those who had murdered Darnley, who did all they could to keep the truth from her, Mary's bewilderment and grief began to affect her health, and her council persuaded her to take a break at Seaton House, a country residence she was fond of only seven miles from Edinburgh. She went there on 16 February, but ironically, her entourage included Argyll, Huntly, Bothwell, Arbroath, the Archbishop of St Andrews, Lords Fleming and Livingston, and Secretary Maitland

At Seaton, Mary entered into correspondence with the Earl of Lennox, Darnley's father. His first letter, dated 20 February 1567, thanked her for her efforts so far to find the culprits, but since they had been fruitless he begged her to assemble the nobility to help in her investigations. Mary's reply the next day informed him that shortly before receiving his letter she had ordered parliament to convene to consider the matter. Lennox wrote back on 26 February to explain that he had not meant to suggest she hold a full parliament. He had heard of the placards set up in Edinburgh, which had named certain persons as the murderers, and he asked her to have the authors arrested and brought before the nobility and Privy Council to confront those whom they had accused. If they refused to appear or could not prove their charges, the accused would be exonerated.

Mary realized that this proposal was unconstitutional, and if she imprisoned everyone accused in anonymous bills, law and justice would degenerate into despotism or civil anarchy. In her letter of 1 March she informed Lennox that although parliament would have to consider the matter, her lords and Privy Council would pursue it in the mean time. As for his request that the persons named in the placards be apprehended, the claims were too unreliable and contradictory to justify throwing any of her subjects into prison, but if he would name those whom he thought should face trial, she would order it immediately. She was anxious for Lennox to take responsibility for this himself because up to now she had been kept very much in the dark and needed the help of someone as keen as she was to discover the truth.

Lennox's reply on 17 March expressed his surprise that the identity of those whom the placards accused had been kept from her, and he named them himself, beginning with the Earl of Bothwell. He admitted he had no evidence of their guilt but said he greatly suspected Bothwell and hoped she would act on the information. Mary had returned to Edinburgh by this time and wrote back to Lennox immediately, saying she had summoned her nobility to Edinburgh the first week of April, when those named in his letter would be committed for trial, and she invited Lennox to attend and lend his assistance.

It was a bold move to arraign a nobleman so powerful and well respected as Bothwell on such vague evidence of such a serious crime, but if Mary exceeded the limits of her constitutional authority, it was understandable in the circumstances. She summoned her Privy Council immediately after receiving Lennox's last letter and laid it before them. The trial of Bothwell and the others named by Lennox was fixed for 12 April 1567, and proclamations were made in Edinburgh, Glasgow, Dumbarton and other places calling on all who wanted to accuse Bothwell or his accomplices to appear in court on that day. However, because the only evidence so far was the anonymous placards, the council refused to imprison the suspects in the mean time.

The Earl of Lennox immediately set out for Edinburgh from his Dunbartonshire estate, via Stirling, avoiding the direct route for fear of reprisals from Bothwell. Bothwell, however, had decided to rely on the help of his friends among the nobility. Having removed all who might have been witnesses against him, he brought into Edinburgh a large body of retainers and decided to brazen out the accusation with his usual audacity. Assuming the air of an injured and innocent man, he complained of unfair treatment. The only grounds for accusing him were a bill posted anonymously on the Tolbooth and he had been allowed only fifteen days rather than the usual forty to prepare his defence.

The day of the trial was drawing near, but to her astonishment, the day before it was to take place Mary received a letter from the Earl of Lennox in Stirling, saying he was uncertain how to proceed, requesting a postponement on grounds of ill health and lack of time to prepare his case, and asking for the suspects to be taken into custody until the rescheduled trial took place. Mary was deeply disappointed. Postponing the trial without the accused's consent was out of the question, and if Lennox needed more time, why hadn't he asked for it as soon as the trial date had been announced? If

she postponed it now, it might never take place, and her enemies would find fault with whatever she decided – if she
proceeded, they would accuse her of too much haste; if she
postponed, they would accuse her of indifference. In a letter
written on 8 April, unlikely to reach Mary until the morning
of the trial at the very earliest, Elizabeth went so far as to
suggest that suspicion might fall on Mary herself unless she
complied with Lennox's request to postpone the trial. The
truth was that as soon as she heard of Darnley's death, Elizabeth had eagerly considered the possibility of implicating her
sister queen in his murder and she was the first to attempt
openly to sow such a suspicion in the minds of Mary's subjects.

Bothwell's trial was held on Saturday 12 April 1567 in Edinburgh Tolbooth. Lord High Justice the Earl of Argyll presided, attended by four legal advisers, two of them, James
MacGill and Henry Balnaves, Senators of the College of Justice, the third Robert Pitcairn, Commendator of Dunfermline, and the fourth Lord Lindsay. The indictment accused
Bothwell of being 'art and part of the cruel, odious, treasonable, and abominable slaughter and murder, of the umwhile
the Right High and Mighty Prince the King's Grace, dearest
spouse for the time to our Sovereign Lady the Queen's Majesty'.

Bothwell appeared at the bar, supported by the Earl of
Morton and two gentlemen who were to act as his advocates. However, although there were frequent calls for the
Earl of Lennox or other accusers to come forward, none appeared. Finally, Robert Cunningham, one of Lennox's servants, stepped forward and produced a note from his master

explaining that the cause of Lennox's absence was shortness of time and the lack of friends and retainers to accompany him to the trial, and that he therefore objected to any decision the court might come to. In response to this protest, Lennox's letters to the queen asking for speedy action against the suspects were produced and read, and Bothwell's counsel argued that the trial should proceed immediately, according to the laws of the realm and the wishes of the accused. The judges agreed that Bothwell had a right to insist on the trial proceeding, so a jury was chosen. It did not include many of Bothwell's friends, consisting of the Earls of Rothes, Caithness and Cassilis, Lord John Hamilton, son of the Duke of Chatelherault, Lords Ross, Semple, Herries, Oliphant and Boyd, the Master of Forbes, Gordon of Lochinvar, Cockburn of Langton, Sommerville of Cambusnethan, Mowbray of Barnbougle and Ogilvy of Boyne. Bothwell pled not guilty, and since no evidence was presented against him, the jury immediately retired for some time. When they returned, their verdict, delivered by their foreman, the Earl of Caithness, unanimously acquitted Bothwell of murdering the king.

Immediately after his acquittal, Bothwell, as was customary in those times, published a challenge in which he offered to fight hand to hand with any man who declared that he still suspected him of having played a role in the king's death, but nobody accepted. His position was now stronger than ever, and he could claim that whoever was guilty, it could not be him since he had been found innocent in a court of law. He attended the parliament that met on 14 April in triumph with a large body of retainers and banners flying, and an Act was passed making it a criminal offence not only to put up any placards defaming the nobility but to fail to destroy them as soon as they appeared. Although overshadowed by recent events, this parliament also passed an Act renouncing all foreign jurisdiction in ecclesiastical affairs and allowing all Mary's subjects to worship God in their own way.

Moray attended neither the trial nor the parliament. Mary had given him permission to leave Scotland, and on 9 April he set off for France, visiting London and Elizabeth's court on the way. He was probably concerned that if the current turbulence led to civil war, he would be obliged to take sides immediately and might again find himself on the losing one. He may not have been aware of Bothwell's more ambitious plans, but having given tacit approval to the king's murder, probably hoping the plot would go wrong and lead to Bothwell's downfall, he had decided that if he kept his distance for a while he could choose his moment to intervene and gain in popularity and power.

CHAPTER VI

ABDUCTION OF A QUEEN

Bothwell's plans were going well, and he now had Mary's hand and Scotland's crown within his grasp. But could Mary be persuaded to accept him as a husband? The unsettled state of the country would no doubt convince her that she needed a strong consort to help her keep her turbulent subjects in order, and she would probably feel that one of her own nobility would be the best candidate. However, he felt she was unlikely to choose him. It was true she had recently given him considerable responsibility in the administration, but he felt this reflected a desire to preserve a balance of power between himself and her other ministers rather than any personal regard. His best efforts to endear himself to Mary had failed – although she valued him as a faithful officer of state, his coarse manners and dissolute habits made him unattractive to her. Bothwell therefore decided that he would have to resort to fraud and perhaps force.

Parliament only continued until 19 April 1567, and the following evening Bothwell invited nearly all the lords who were in Edinburgh to a great supper in a tavern kept by a man called Ainsly, which later led to the occasion being known as 'Ainsly's Supper'. After plying his guests with wine, he produced a document he had drawn up and asked them all to sign it. It was in the form of a bond, and in the preamble, after expressing the conviction that Bothwell had been grossly slandered by being accused of being party to Darnley's murder and that his innocence had been proved at his trial, they agreed that they would take firm and resolute action against any person or persons who repeated the slander.

After this introduction, which evidently aimed to remove any lingering suspicion Mary might have of Bothwell's guilt, the bond went on to state: 'Moreover, weighing and considering the present time, and how our Sovereign, the Queen's Majesty, is destitute of a husband, in which solitary state the common weal of this realm may not permit her Highness to continue and endure, but at some time her Highness, in appearance, may be inclined to yield unto a marriage – therefore, in case the former affectionate and hearty services of the said Earl [Bothwell], done to her Majesty from time to time, and his other good qualities and behaviour, may move her Majesty so far to humble herself as, preferring one of her own native born subjects unto all foreign princes, to take to husband the said Earl, we, and every one of us under subscribing, upon our honours and fidelity, oblige ourselves, and promise, not only to further, advance, and set forward the marriage to be solemnized and completed betwixt her Highness and the said noble Lord, with our votes, counsel, fortification and assistance, in word and deed, at such time as it shall please her Majesty to think it convenient, and as soon as the laws shall permit it to be done; but, in case any should presume, directly or indirectly, openly, or under whatsoever colour or pretence, to hinder, hold back, or disturb the same marriage, we shall, in that behalf, hold and repute the hinderers, adversaries, or disturbers thereof, as our common enemies and evil-willers; and notwithstanding the same, take part with, and fortify the said Earl to the said marriage so far as it may please our said Sovereign Lady to allow; and therein shall spend and bestow our lives and goods against all that live or die, as we shall answer to God, and upon our own fidelities and conscience; and in case we do the contrary, never to have reputation or credit in no time hereafter, but to be accounted unworthy and faithless traitors.'

All the nobles present signed it, except the Earl of Eglinton, who had slipped away unnoticed, and among the signatories were the Archbishop of St Andrews, the Bishops of Aberdeen, Dunblane, Brechin and Ross, the Earls of Huntly, Argyll, Morton, Cassilis, Sutherland, Errol, Crawford, Caithness and Rothes, and the Lords Boyd, Glamis, Ruthven, Semple, Herries, Ogilvie and Fleming. Bothwell might have had good reason to doubt the sincerity of many of the subscribers, and there is no way so many lords would have signed such a bond on the spur of the moment, so it must have been the culmination of a great deal of behind-the-scenes bargaining by Bothwell, first persuading Morton, his brother-in-law Huntly, Argyll and others, and then using their influence to win over others. Once a large enough majority had agreed to sign, the rest would fall into line, fearing the consequences of refusal if Bothwell ever became king. Bothwell was worried about presenting Mary with the bond openly since her aversion to marrying him might have outweighed even the almost unanimous recommendation of her nobility, but having come this far, he was not about to allow a woman's will to present a serious obstacle to his ambition.

For a short while the supper's proceedings were concealed from Mary, and although Bothwell's intentions became the subject of much discussion throughout the country, she was the last to hear of them. When Lord Herries mentioned to Mary that there were rumours she was thinking of marrying Bothwell, Mary marvelled at such nonsense and said she had no such thing in mind.

Only a day or two after the bond was signed, the queen was due to leave Edinburgh to visit her son, who was being looked after by the Earl of Mar at Stirling. Before she went, Bothwell finally plucked up the courage to propose to her. Mary's response was disappointing, but he was not prepared to take 'no' for an answer.

Mary was to return from Stirling on 24 April, so Bothwell left Edinburgh with a force of nearly a thousand well-mounted men under the pretext of going off to quell some riots in the Borders. However, they had travelled only a few miles south when they suddenly turned west, rode with all speed to Linlithgow and waited for Mary at a bridge over the River Almond about a mile from the town.

The queen soon appeared with a small entourage, which was easily overpowered by the vastly superior force. The Earl of Huntly, Secretary Maitland and Sir James Melville, the only persons of rank who were accompanying the queen, were taken captive along with her, but the rest of her attendants were dismissed. Bothwell himself seized the bridle of Mary's horse and, turning off the road to Edinburgh, hurried with her to his castle at Dunbar.

Bothwell kept Mary in near-solitary confinement in Dunbar Castle for ten days. She hoped that some of her more loyal nobles would try to free her, but none did, for Bothwell was either dreaded by, or in league with, all of them. Bothwell took his opportunity to declare to her that he would make her his wife, no matter who objected and whether she agreed or not. Mary replied by accusing him of the foulest ingratitude and said his conduct grieved her all the more because he was the last person she would have expected to have done this. Bothwell stayed with her all day long, constantly trying to persuade her.

Sometimes he would fling himself at her feet and beg her to pardon an act that had been prompted by the strength of his love for her, bemoaning the fact that his enemies, with no provocation on his part, were always conspiring against him, even accusing him of murdering the king. He could not even trust those who pretended to be his friends, and the only way he could find security would be if she took him as her husband. He declared that he would not, as Darnley had done, seek to usurp her but would continue to be her loyal servant as before. At other times he would fly into a rage and threaten dishonour, imprisonment and death if she refused to comply with his demands.

Nearly a week into her ordeal, to try to give the impression that Mary was staying at Dunbar voluntarily, he called together a few of the lords of the Privy Council on whom he could depend, and on 29 April they passed an unimportant Act concerning provisions for the royal household. Given his current influence over the Scottish nobles, Bothwell could have held a Privy Council at Dunbar every day if he had wished, and whether he had allowed the queen to be present or not, nobody would have objected to anything he proposed. Meanwhile, mutual divorce proceedings between Bothwell and his wife, Lady Jane Gordon, were being hurried through the courts, and they were granted in a few days.

On 3 May 1567, Bothwell decided to take Mary from Dunbar to Edinburgh Castle under close guard. When they approached the town, he told his followers to conceal their weapons to avoid anyone realizing that the queen was his prisoner. The truth came out in spite of his precautions – at the foot of the Canongate, Mary was about to turn her horse towards Holyrood when Bothwell seized the bridle and led her up the High Street to the castle, which was in the charge of Sir James Balfour, one of Bothwell's lackeys.

Having finally gained Mary's reluctant consent by means that remain a mystery but were rumoured to include raping her, Bothwell was determined that the marriage should go ahead as soon as possible. Mary may have had little choice but to agree to marry him, but she refused to help in the arrangements. Three days after she arrived at the castle, Thomas Hepburn (probably a relation of the Hepburn who was engaged with Bothwell in Darnley's murder) was sent to ask Craig, Knox's colleague in the Church of St Giles, to proclaim the banns of matrimony between the queen and Bothwell, but Craig refused because Hepburn brought no authority from the queen.

In a day or two, the Lord Justice Clerk conveyed the written mandate to Craig, but the preacher still had some scruples. Feeling that the marriage contravened the laws of both God and man, he insisted on seeing the queen and Bothwell before he published the banns. He was admitted to a meeting of the Privy Council where Bothwell presided but Mary was not present. Craig later reported: 'In the Council, I laid to his charge the law of adultery, the ordinance of the kirk, the law of ravishing, the suspicion of collusion betwixt him and his wife, the sudden divorcement and proclaiming within the space of four days, and lastly, the suspicion of the King's death, which his marriage would confirm; but he answered nothing to my satisfaction. . . . Therefore, upon Sunday, after I had declared what they had done, and how they would proceed, whether we would or not, I took heaven and earth to witness, that I abhorred and detested that marriage, because it was odious and scandalous to the world; and seeing the best part of the realm did approve it, either by flattery or by their silence, I desired the faithful to pray earnestly, that God would turn it to the comfort of this realm.'

Bothwell did not allow the queen to leave the castle until 12 May, after the banns had been proclaimed twice. He took her to the Court of Session, where he persuaded her to sign two deeds of great importance to him. When the lords had signed the bond at Ainsly's Supper they had not imagined that Bothwell would resort to violence to persuade her, and they were worried that the queen might think they were implicated in an act that many of them secretly viewed with disgust. As a precaution, therefore, they required Bothwell to obtain a written promise from the queen that she would never deem their consent to the bond a criminal act.

On the same day, before the Lords of Session and others, Mary granted a formal pardon to Bothwell for his recent conduct. It states: 'That albeit her Highness was commoved for the present time of her taking at the said Earl Bothwell; yet for his good behaviour, and thankful service in time past, and for more thankful service in time coming, her Highness stands content with the said Earl, and has forgiven and forgives him, and all others his accomplices, being with him in company at the time, all hatred conceived by her Majesty, for the taking and imprisoning of her, at the time foresaid.'

The appointment of Bothwell as Duke of Orkney meant that preparations for the wedding were complete, but even the conduct of the marriage ceremony illustrates the despotic power Bothwell now wielded over Mary. She had never before failed to observe the rites of her own faith, however tolerant she was to those of a different persuasion, but now had to submit to be married according to the Protestant rite. Adam Bothwell, Bishop of Orkney, who had recently converted from Episcopalianism and joined the Reformers, presided over the ceremony, which was held in the Council Chamber. After the sermon, the congregation dispersed with few signs of celebration.

When Melville came to court that evening, he found Bothwell in his cups, sitting at the supper table with Huntly, the Justice Clerk and others: 'He said I had been a great stranger, desiring me to sit down and sup with him. I said that I had already supped. Then he called for a cup of wine, and drank to me, that I might pledge him like a Dutchman. He made me drink it out to grow fatter, "for," said he, "the zeal of the commonweal has eaten ye up, and made ye lean." I answered, that every little member should serve to some use; but that the care of the commonweal appertained most to him, and the rest of the nobility, who should be as fathers to it. Then he said, I well knew he would find a pin for every bore. Then he discoursed of gentlewomen, speaking such filthy language, that I left him, and passed up to the Queen, who was very glad at my coming.'

Bothwell persuaded Mary to send ambassadors to the courts of England and France to explain the reasons for their marriage, including Bothwell's services to both Mary and her mother, his influence in Scotland, his popularity among the nobility and their strong desire that he should become king. Although Mary signed the ambassadors' instructions, they were no doubt drafted by Bothwell's friend, Secretary Maitland, and the account they gave of his recent conduct was designed to give the impression that the queen could not have chosen a better husband.

Now resigned to her marriage, Mary was determined to protect and be loyal to her husband, but those close to her could see she was miserable. So little love existed between them that even the days usually set aside for nuptial celebrations were marked only by suspicion and wrangling. They remained together at Holyrood from 10 May to 7 June, but Bothwell was so concerned that she might still break free and assert her independence that he kept her under constant armed guard, and if anyone wished an audience with her the ranks of two hundred men armed with handguns had to be negotiated. Bothwell's suspicious nature and troubled conscience meant that very few were admitted to her presence anyway.

Although Bothwell had divorced his first wife, this was merely part of his scheme to gain the throne, and his attachment to Lady Jane Gordon continued unabated. Regarded with suspicion by foreign royalty, virtually a prisoner in her own realm, hated by many of her more bigoted Presbyterian subjects and subject to brutal treatment from her worthless husband, in her bleaker moments Mary even contemplated suicide. Her heart was broken, the outlook was grim, and her precious honour was in doubt. She was a queen who lacked authority over her subjects and a wife who lacked the love of her husband. The humblest peasant in Scotland was to be envied more than the daughter of the royal line.

But there was trouble in store for Bothwell. Many, even his own friends, felt that he had acted too high-handedly. They would have been content if he had won Mary by fair means, but not by foul, and when they realized that he had not only forced her to marry him but was rapidly taking absolute power in Scotland, they feared for the constitution and the safety of the Commonweal.

Drunk with power, Bothwell no longer bothered to court the goodwill of those who might be helpful to him or disguise his intentions. He let his closer associates know that if he could get hold of the young Prince James, he would prevent him avenging his father's death. The prince was lodged in Stirling Castle in the custody of the faithful Earl of Mar, who steadfastly refused to deliver him up. The queen was anxious that he remain there, and Bothwell's ceaseless cajoling and threatening began to arouse suspicion and anger throughout Scotland.

A number of the nobility, including Argyll, Atholl, Morton, Mar and Glencairn, met at Stirling and formed an association known as the 'Prince's Lords' to act as his bodyguard – and they soon felt the need to take active measures. On 28

May, proclamations were issued at Edinburgh that the queen and Bothwell intended to set out with a strong force to suppress some disturbances in the Borders and requiring all loyal subjects to assemble in arms at Melrose. It was immediately rumoured that this expedition was only a pretence and that Bothwell's real intention was to march to Stirling and take possession of the castle and its inhabitants. A second proclamation tried to dismiss this suspicion as unfounded, but many remained unconvinced, and the Prince's Lords busied themselves collecting their followers, as if complying with the order to assemble at Melrose.

Bothwell had reason to suspect that Sir James Balfour, the governor of Edinburgh Castle, was secretly in league with the Prince's Lords and might be persuaded to storm Holyrood with a party of troops and imprison him in the castle. Since Edinburgh was no longer safe for him, on 6 or 7 June Bothwell took the queen from Holyrood Palace to Borthwick Castle, eight miles to the south of Edinburgh. Once the Prince's Lords heard of Bothwell's retreat, they decided to take advantage of it. Advancing unexpectedly from Stirling, they marched past Edinburgh and surrounded Borthwick Castle, but Bothwell and the queen managed to escape to Dunbar, so the Prince's Lords fell back to Edinburgh. Although Bothwell's ally Huntly was in command of the city, they had little difficulty forcing their way through the city gates. Huntly and the rest of Bothwell's friends, thinking that Balfour was still in league with them, retreated into the castle. The Prince's Lords, headed by Morton, immediately issued proclamations demanding the assistance of all loyal subjects on the grounds that 'the Queen's Majesty, being detained in captivity, was neither able to govern her realm, nor try the murder of her husband, and that they had assembled to deliver her and preserve the Prince'.

Another proclamation, issued at Edinburgh on 12 June, shows that Bothwell's guilt and the circumstances of the marriage were now public knowledge: 'The Lords of Secret Council and Nobility, understanding that James, Earl of Bothwell, put violent hands on our Sovereign Lady's most noble person upon the 24th day of April last, and thereafter warded [imprisoned] her Highness in the Castle of Dunbar, which he had in keeping, and, before a long space thereafter, conveyed her Majesty, environed with men of war, and such friends and kinsmen of his as would do for him, ever into such places where he had most dominion and power, her Grace being destitute of all counsel and servants, during which time the said Earl seduced, by unlawful ways, our said Sovereign to a dishonest marriage with himself, which, from the beginning is null and of no effect.' The proclamation ended by announcing their determination to free the queen and bring Bothwell and his accomplices to trial, both for the murder of Darnley and for 'the ravishing and detaining of the Queen's Majesty's person', as well as to prevent them harming the prince.

Meanwhile, Bothwell was gathering his forces at Dunbar. In a few days, more than two thousand men had joined up, more because the queen was with him than from any loyalty to himself. Fearing that the Prince's Lords were also gathering strength, he marched from Dunbar with this army on 14 June. When the news of his approach reached Edinburgh the Prince's Lords, although they had fewer troops, immediately advanced to meet him. The two armies did not come into view of each other until the next morning, when Bothwell's troops were sighted on Carberry Hill, between Musselburgh and Dalkeith. Having spent the night at Musselburgh, the Prince's Lords made a circuit towards Dalkeith to gain the high ground and took up position to the west of Bothwell's troops.

Neither party was in a hurry to enter battle, and the French ambassador, Le Croc, spent several hours riding between both armies trying to broker an agreement. The queen had authorized him to promise that the current insurrection would be willingly forgiven if they laid down their arms and disbanded their followers. Morton replied that they had taken up arms not against the queen but against the king's murderer, and if she delivered him to be punished, or at least separated from him, they would gladly disband.

In despair at the impasse, Le Croc returned to Edinburgh. Both parties continued to play for time, Bothwell because he was expecting reinforcements from Lord Herries and others, and the Prince's Lords because they also hoped others would join them, and furthermore it was hot and the sun was shining strongly in their faces. As a delaying tactic, Bothwell offered to resolve the quarrel by taking on any lord of equal rank in single combat. Kirkcaldy of Grange, one of the best soldiers of the day, and Murray of Tullibardine were both willing to accept the challenge but were rejected because of their inferior rank, so Lord Lindsay came forward. Bothwell had no grounds for refusal, and despite the fact that their army was superior to their opponents', Mary gave her consent. Twenty gentlemen on either side were to attend, and the ground was about to be marked out when the Prince's Lords changed their minds and declared themselves unwilling that Lindsay should take upon himself the whole burden of a quarrel in which they all felt equally interested.

These negotiations lasted until 7 p.m., and there might have been a battle either that night or next morning had the queen not taken an unexpected step. Although unwilling to betray Bothwell directly, she was determined to escape from his clutches. Many of those with her at Carberry Hill that day suspected she had already made a secret arrangement with the Prince's Lords and felt it understandable in view of Bothwell's mistreatment of her. She had suffered many indignities at his hands since their marriage, and not a day had passed without him reducing her to tears, so even some of his own company detested him, and others believed that the queen would have been glad to be rid of him but needed a face-saving pretext. She summoned Kirkcaldy of Grange and told him she was willing to part from Bothwell as they demanded if Morton and the other lords would promise to conduct her safely to Edinburgh and resume allegiance to her. Kirkcaldy immediately accepted these terms as long as Mary agreed to dismiss Bothwell there and then.

So determined was Bothwell to stay and make good use of his superior forces that when he overheard these negotiations he ordered a soldier to shoot Kirkcaldy, but Mary finally persuaded him to mount his horse and ride away with a few followers back to Dunbar. As soon as her husband had left, Mary mounted her own horse and asked Kirkcaldy to take her horse's bridle and lead her to the Prince's Lords. When Morton and the rest came forward to meet her, receiving her with all due respect, she said to them: 'My Lords, I am come to you, not out of any fear I had of my life, nor yet doubting of the victory, if matters had gone to the worst; but I abhor the shedding of Christian blood, especially of those that are my own subjects; and therefore I yield to you, and will be ruled hereafter by your counsels, trusting you will respect me as your born Princess and Queen.'

This was a big mistake. Mary did not realize the kind of men she had just surrendered herself to, nor did she anticipate that their hired retainers, having been cheated of a battle, might take revenge by insulting the Roman Catholic sovereign who was now practically their prisoner.

When they led her into Edinburgh between 8 and 9 p.m. that evening, the citizens had already heard the news of what had happened. Great crowds lined the way as they passed, but this was no triumphal procession for Mary. A banner at the front of the cavalcade showed Darnley lying dead at the foot of a tree and the young prince on his knees near him, exclaiming: 'Judge and revenge my cause, O Lord!' The more zealous and less honest among the Presbyterians had long resented Mary's sovereignty, and rebellious and unprincipled voices led the mob's shouts of savage glee as this ensign was carried past, heaping scornful insults on Mary, who rode on in tears. Far from being allowed to return to Edinburgh as queen to resume her throne, Mary was being exhibited like a captive. The hatred people felt towards Bothwell had been transferred to her, and the Prince's Lords, headed by the crafty Morton, had delivered her from one tyrant only to place her in the hands of many.

When Mary realized she was not being taken to Holyrood

111

House, she called on anyone who came near to rescue her from the traitors. The mob was too excited to pay any attention, so she was lodged in the provost's house in the High Street for the night. The crowd gradually dispersed, and the lords were left to plan what to do next.

Morton once more had the queen in his custody, and, thinking he had the support of the public, he set out to win Elizabeth's lasting gratitude and perhaps secure the regency of Scotland for himself. Kirkcaldy of Grange was the only lord to express doubts about their conduct. He reminded them that he had promised the queen their loyalty as long as she parted from Bothwell and came over to their side, and since she had fulfilled her part of the bargain, he felt it wrong not to honour theirs. Seeing that his argument might sow dissent among the lords, Morton produced a letter from Mary to Bothwell, which he claimed he had just intercepted and in which she declared that she would never abandon Bothwell, although for a time she might be obliged to yield to circumstances. Kirkcaldy, an honest and trusting type, was shocked by the forged letter and abandoned his defence of the queen.

But Morton had been overconfident. After a night's reflection, the ever-fluctuating populace had begun to entertain some doubts. The next morning they gathered in front of the provost's house, and after the queen had come to the window several times to protest that her own nobles had betrayed her and were holding her prisoner, public opinion began to change in her favour. Morton and his colleagues realized what was happening and with the utmost hypocrisy told the queen that she had quite mistaken their intentions, and to convince her of their sincerity they would immediately reinstate her in Holyrood Palace. Mary was deceived once more. That evening, pretending to fulfil their promise, they took her to Holyrood, Morton walking respectfully on one side of her horse and Atholl on the other, but once she arrived at the palace she realized she was still being watched over as closely as ever. To add insult to injury, the lords had stolen much of her valuable furniture.

Around midnight, to her terror and surprise, a group of lords suddenly removed her from her chamber. They forced her to disguise herself in an ordinary riding habit and then ride off under escort by Lords Ruthven and Lindsay without telling her where they were taking her.

Early next morning they arrived at Loch Leven Castle, a formidable stronghold on a small island in the centre of the loch, the shortest approach from the shore being about half a mile. The castle belonged to Lady Douglas – Lady Loch Leven, as she was commonly called – the widow of Sir Robert Douglas and mother of the Earl of Moray by James V. The castle's situation and the fact it was owned by a close relative of a number of the Prince's Lords made it ideal for its present purpose. Lady Loch Leven did not disappoint the lords, taunting the captive queen with her misfortune and bragging that she herself was King James V's lawful wife, and her son, the Earl of Moray, was his legitimate issue and true heir to the crown.

Morton and his friends tried to justify their actions by passing an Act of Privy Council, but they had difficulty deciding how to frame it in view of the proclamations in the queen's favour that they had so recently signed and the solemn agreement they had entered into at Carberry Hill. To

113

protect themselves from accusations of treason, they claimed that although they still believed the queen had married Bothwell unwillingly and been his prisoner, and although she had agreed to separate from him at Carberry, she was strongly opposed to seeking punishment for Darnley's murderers, implying that her support for Bothwell and his accomplices drew suspicion on herself.

However, a bond of association that they drew up the same day directly contradicts the Act of Council, containing no accusations against Mary and representing her throughout as the victim of force and fraud. It accused Bothwell of Darnley's murder, taking Mary prisoner at Dunbar Castle, marrying her unlawfully, keeping her in 'shameful thraldom' and threatening the young prince – these were the reasons for the lords banding together against Bothwell, and having ousted him from his unlawful authority, they felt obliged to continue in arms until 'the authors of the murder and ravishing were condignly punished, the pretended marriage dissolved, their sovereign relieved of the thraldom, bondage, and ignominy, which she had sustained, and still underlies by the said Earl's fault, the person of the innocent prince placed in safety, and, finally, justice restored and uprightly administered to all the subjects of the realm'.

Morton and the other lords claimed they had sent Mary to Loch Leven merely to keep her safe from Bothwell, and as soon as they had captured him or driven him from the kingdom, they would restore her to the throne. They made no mention of the theory that Mary had colluded in Darnley's murder, expressly declaring that Bothwell alone was to blame for everything.

The overall impression they gave was that they were as loyal to the queen as ever, that they intended her to remain at Loch Leven for only a short while and that, far from intending to force her to abdicate and imprison her for the rest of her life, they would soon rally around her and bring her back to the capital in triumph. Some among their number may indeed have entertained these hopes, but they did not take into account the fact that Morton had already assassinated Rizzio and agreed to the murder of Darnley, and that Moray, currently in France, had left the country only until new disturbances would give him an opportunity to further his own ambitions.

CHAPTER VII

$\mathcal{M}$ARY AT LOCH LEVEN

Scotland was now in turmoil, and the nobility was divided into two factions. The largest party, the Queen's Lords, based at Hamilton Palace, included the Hamiltons, Huntly (whom Balfour had allowed to escape from Edinburgh Castle), Argyll (who had earlier joined the Prince's Lords but had never intended taking up arms against the queen), Rothes, Caithness, Crawford, Boyd, Herries, Livingston, Seaton and Ogilvie. Through the mediation of the General Assembly, Morton, as head of the Prince's Lords, tried to form a coalition with some of the Queen's Lords, but they would have none of it. At this time Mary may have had more friends than enemies, but unfortunately they were unable to form a united front in her defence.

Morton did all he could to try to increase the popularity of his faction. He arrested several people whom he accused of being accomplices in Darnley's murder, and although he probably knew they were innocent, they were all condemned and executed, with the exception of Sebastian, the queen's servant, who was seized in order to cast suspicion on Mary herself but who managed to escape.

For his own reasons, Morton was more cautious in his

treatment of Bothwell. Not until 26 June was the keeper of Dunbar Castle, who was protecting Bothwell, ordered to deliver up his charge, and on the same day a proclamation was issued offering the moderate reward of 1,000 crowns to anyone who apprehended the earl.

After he fled from Dunbar, little is known of Bothwell's movements and actions, but he went north, where he had estates as Duke of Orkney and some influence with his kinsman, the Bishop of Moray. Sir William Kirkcaldy of Grange and Tullibardine were allocated several ships and sent to pursue him, but Bothwell was forewarned and escaped to Orkney and Shetland, where he was very nearly captured. At one point Kirkcaldy and Tullibardine's ships were within gunshot of Bothwell's, and they would have captured him had their vessels not collided with a sunken rock. They did manage to seize some of his accomplices, who were taken back to Edinburgh. Their confessions revealed the details of the murder plot, and they were tried and condemned.

Bothwell decided to take refuge in Denmark, hoping that King Frederick II, a distant relation of Mary's through her great-grandmother, Margaret of Denmark, the wife of James III, might help him. He felt he needed to make an impressive entrance to the Danish court, so to increase his funds he seized one or two merchant vessels trading in the North Sea. When this came to light he was arrested and taken to Denmark, not as an exiled prince but as a captive pirate, and thrown into prison. When he revealed his identity the Danes were unimpressed. He remained in prison for many years, the King of Denmark unwilling to surrender him to Elizabeth or his enemies in Scotland but having no wish to offend them by setting him free. A broken man, Bothwell is believed to have been mentally deranged in his last years, and he died in misery.

Meanwhile, foreign courts were concerned about the state of affairs in Scotland. An ambassador arrived from Mary's friends in France, but finding to his astonishment that she was a prisoner and some of the nobility had usurped the government, he refused to acknowledge their authority and immediately left the country.

Elizabeth was delighted with the turn of events, and the letters she sent via her ambassador, Sir Nicholas Throckmorton, reveal the depth of her duplicity, mock sincerity and real heartlessness. Throckmorton brought with him two distinct sets of 'Instructions', both dated 30 June 1567, one to be shown to Mary and the other to the rebel lords.

The set addressed to Mary expressed the greatest indignation at her imprisonment and threatened vengeance on all her enemies. Nevertheless, despite declarations to the contrary by the rebel lords, Elizabeth chose to believe that Mary had consented to the hasty marriage with Bothwell and that she therefore shared his guilt. She proposed that Mary should be freed on condition that she immediately prosecuted and punished Darnley's murderers and guaranteed the young prince's safety – but how could Mary punish murderers who had yet to be identified or arrested, and who could imagine she would wish to harm her only son?

The set addressed to the rebel lords told them that if Elizabeth were allowed to mediate between their queen and them, 'they should have no just cause to mislike her doings', because her first concern was 'for their security hereafter, and for quietness to the realm'. Throckmorton was instructed to assure them that she 'meant not to allow of such faults as she hears by report are imputed to the Queen of Scots, but had given him strictly in charge to lay before, and to reprove her, in her name, for the same . . . we mean not with any such partiality to deal for her, but that her princely state being preserved, she should conform herself to all reasonable devices that may bring a good accord betwixt her and her nobility and people'. Morton and his colleagues realized that for the sake of appearances Elizabeth had to pretend to disapprove of their actions, but in reality she was well pleased with them.

The rebel lords drew up a state paper to explain recent events to Throckmorton. It contained no suspicion of the queen being implicated in Bothwell's guilt and insisted that she married him very unwillingly and only after force had been used, but they made certain allegations to justify imprisoning her. An hour or two after parting from her husband at Carberry Hill, they claimed, having come with them to Edinburgh voluntarily, she suffered a change of heart and they 'found her passion so prevail in maintenance of him and his cause, that she would not with patience hear speak any thing to his reproof, or suffer his doings to be called in question; but, on the contrary, offered to give over the realm and all, so that she might be suffered to enjoy him, with many threatenings to be revenged on every man who had dealt in the matter'. But the same paper also claimed that 'the Queen, their Sovereign, had been led captive, and, by fear, force, and other extraordinary and more unlawful means, compelled to become bedfellow to another wife's husband', and asserted that even without their intervention, they did not believe she would have stayed with him longer than six months. In conclusion, they assured Throckmorton that, 'knowing the great wisdom wherewith God hath endowed her', they expected that within a short time her mind would be settled, and that as soon as 'by a just trial they had made the truth appear, she would conform herself to their doings'.

Four different schemes were now proposed to resolve the situation. The first, suggested by the Queen's Lords assembled at Hamilton, was to free the queen and restore her to the throne on condition that she promised to pardon the rebel lords, to keep the prince safe from harm, to divorce Bothwell and to punish all those implicated in Darnley's murder. The other three, proposed by Morton and his party, were worthy of their authors. The first called for the queen to abdicate in favour of her son, the country being governed by a council of the nobility while she retired to France or England, never to return. The second suggested the queen be tried and sentenced to life imprisonment, the prince succeeding to the throne. The third and most extreme measure was to have her tried, condemned and executed. Although Elizabeth would probably have approved of the third option, Throckmorton warned them to be careful 'that by their doings they should not wipe away the Queen's infamy, and the Lord Bothwell's detestable murder, and by their outrageous dealings bring all the slander upon themselves'. At Morton's request he suggested that Elizabeth send some 12,000 crowns to help meet the rebel lords' increased expenditure, especially since Maitland of Lethington and others had reminded him that despite all her fair words, Moray, Morton and the rest 'had in their troubles found cold relief and small favour at her Majesty's hands'.

In moments when his better nature prevailed, Throckmorton was disgusted by the role he was forced to play in these negotiations, as he revealed to Melville, reporting that Cecil had proposed openly 'that it was needful for the welfare of England, to foster and nourish the civil wars, as well in France and in Flanders, as in Scotland; whereby England might reap many advantages, and be sought after by all parties, and in the meantime live in rest, and gather great riches. This advice and proposition was well liked by most part of the Council; yet an honest counsellor stood up and said, it was a very worldly advice, and had little or nothing to do with a Christian commonweal.'

In France, Moray was anxiously observing events in his home country, where he wielded as much influence as Morton because some of the Scottish lords had been in close correspondence with him via Cecil. On 26 June, four days before Throckmorton had left London for Scotland, Cecil wrote to the English ambassador in Paris that 'Moray's return into Scotland was much desired, for the weal both of England and Scotland.' Moray had attempted to ingratiate himself with the French court by exaggerating his loyalty to Mary, and the sudden turn of events meant he could not return immediately, so he sent Elphinstone as his emissary. The lords allowed him to visit the queen at Loch Leven, a privilege they had allowed no one else. Morton realized that if Mary abdicated, Moray's popularity in England and Scotland, and in particular with Knox and other preachers, meant that he would have to yield the regency to him, but he consoled himself that he was in great favour with Moray and if he threw in his lot with him he could share in his power and honour.

To prepare the way for Mary's abdication, the lords circulated a report that the queen was still devotedly and almost insanely attached to Bothwell. Throckmorton, who was willing to propagate all the absurd falsehoods they told him, wrote to Elizabeth: 'she avoweth constantly that she will live and die with him; and saith, that if it were put to her choice to relinquish her Crown and kingdom, or the Lord Bothwell, she would leave her kingdom and dignity, to go as a simple damsel with him; and that she will never consent that he shall fare worse, or have more harm than herself.' But the Queen's Lords expressed open disbelief of these reports, and Elizabeth began to fear that she had sent Throckmorton to bargain with the weaker side, later writing to warn him that the doubts the Queen's Lords expressed were unanswerable and there was little hope of convincing them of the truth of Mary's captors' allegations while they were prevented from communicating with her.

It was ridiculous to suggest that Mary refused to return to her throne unless Bothwell joined her, but there may have been some truth in the claim that she currently refused to divorce the man almost all her lords had recommended as a husband and whose child she might be carrying. If she acknowledged that she believed in his guilt, she might implicate herself. She had not married Bothwell until he had been acquitted, and divorcing him before he was tried again could be taken as proof that the trial she had previously sanctioned was just for show.

Nevertheless, the rebel lords pressed ahead with their plans. On 24 July their commissioners, Lord Lindsay and Sir Robert Melville (the brother of Sir James), set off for Loch Leven with three deeds of abdication: the first consisting of Mary's resignation of the crown in favour of her son, the second constituting the Earl of Moray as regent until the prince came of age, and the third appointing a council to administer the government until Moray's return home and, if he refused to accept the regency, until her son was old enough to rule for himself.

The next day, 25 July 1567, must have been one of the worst in Mary's troubled life. Shut up in what was called a castle but was really just a gloomy, square, three-storey tower, attended by only three or four female servants, her misery was about to increase a hundredfold. When she first heard reports that the lords intended to force her to abdicate, she was indignant – was she, descended from a 'centenary line of kings', expected to surrender the crown of the Stuarts into the hands of the bastard Moray or the blood-stained Morton without a struggle?

Melville knew that Mary could not stand Lindsay, so he spoke to her alone at first. He explained why they had come, addressing her with respect and affection, for she had often employed him as a courtier or as her ambassador to foreign courts. As he tried every argument he could muster to persuade her to sign the deeds, she listened with calm dignity and unshaken resolve. He described the state of the nation and insisted she would never again be able to unite it, her enemies being vicious and her friends lukewarm. He told her that if she refused to sign the deeds she would be brought

123

to trial, her character would be besmirched by accusations of
the murder of her late husband and adultery, not only with
Bothwell but with others, and she would almost certainly be
condemned and executed. She remained outwardly unmoved, although she must have felt very bitter at the ingratitude and treachery of those whom she had befriended and
advanced. As a final resort, Melville produced a letter from
Throckmorton advising her to consider her personal safety
and to agree to abdicate, but this rich advice from a man
who supposedly came to Scotland to help restore her to the
throne only made her more suspicious of the sincerity of
Elizabeth's promises of assistance.

Melville now saw that he had no alternative but to call in
Lindsay. Notorious for his vicious temper, he burst into the
queen's presence with the deeds in his hand and rage in his
eyes. Mary was terrified, recalling the evening of Rizzio's
murder, when Lindsay had stood beside the gaunt form of
Ruthven, urging him on. With fearful oaths and curses,
Lindsay vowed that unless she signed the deeds immediately,
he would sign them himself with her blood and seal them on
her heart.

Brave as she was, Mary trembled at this onslaught, and,
thinking that she saw Lindsay's dagger already drawn, she
nearly fainted, bursting into tears. Melville – perhaps to de-
ceive her, perhaps from fear of what Lindsay might do –
whispered in her ear that documents signed in captivity
could not be considered valid if she chose to revoke them
when she regained her liberty. She might have been convinced by this, but before she had time to respond, Lindsay
pointed to the loch and swore that it would be her grave if

she hesitated a moment longer. Driven to distraction and scarcely knowing what she was doing, Mary seized a pen and without reading a line of the deeds signed each of them as well as she could through her tears. The commissioners then took their leave, congratulating themselves that by a mixture of cunning and ferocity they had achieved their aim. Mary, no longer queen, was left alone with her own gloomy thoughts.

As soon as Lindsay returned to Edinburgh to report the success of his mission, Morton and his associates decided that Prince James should be crowned without delay. Sir James Melville, considered a moderate man by both parties, was sent to the Prince's Lords at Hamilton to invite them to attend the coronation. He was received courteously, but they would not agree to the proceedings, which they denounced as treasonable. They moved from Hamilton to Dumbarton, where they prepared for more active opposition. A bond of mutual defence and assistance was drawn up, which declared that owing to the queen's captivity at Loch Leven her subjects were prevented from having free access to her, so it was their duty to free her by any lawful means, whatever the opposition, and it was signed by many persons of rank and influence, including the Archbishop of St Andrews, the Earls of Argyll and Huntly, and Lords Ross, Fleming and Herries.

On 29 July 1567, Prince James, little more than a year old, was publicly crowned at Stirling. He was anointed by Adam, Bishop of Orkney, in the parish church, and the Earl of Morton took the coronation oath in the prince's name. In the procession back to the castle, the Earl of Atholl carried the crown, Morton the sceptre, Glencairn the sword, and Mar the new king. Public writs were issued, and the government was established in the name and authority of James VI. The infant king was in the power of his mother's deadliest enemies, and they were determined that he would share neither her religion nor her opinions, so George Buchanan was appointed his principal tutor, ensuring that Mary would lose not only her crown but her son's love.

A few days after the coronation, Moray returned to Scotland via London, where he drew up plans for the future with Cecil and Elizabeth. He had some difficulty deciding what to do next. He knew he was about to be offered the regency, but he also knew how unlawfully his sister's abdication had been obtained, and that she still enjoyed a good deal of support in Scotland. If he chose to side with the wrong faction he risked losing everything, so he decided, with his usual caution, to feel his way before he took any decisive step.

Sir James Melville was sent to meet him at Berwick, and he learned from him that by this time even Morton's lords had split into two factions, and that while one half was of the opinion that Moray should accept the regency without delay and give his approval to all that had been done in his absence, the other, among whom were Mar, Atholl, Maitland of Lethington, Tullibardine and Kirkcaldy, wanted him to be gentle with the queen and seek her favour if possible, as the time might come when they would want her to rule again.

Moray felt he needed a clearer idea of the state of affairs and public feeling in Scotland, so he decided to visit Mary at Loch Leven, accompanied by Atholl, Morton and Lindsay. When Mary saw her brother she burst into tears, and it was some time before she could speak. She asked the others to leave them alone, and they then had a long private discussion. Mary had flattered herself that she could rely on Moray's affection and gratitude, but she seriously misread his character. Having decided by this time to accept the regency whatever happened, his only desire was to make her believe that he was doing so principally to save her from a worse fate, and that he was doing her a favour. Mary listened to Moray with tears in her eyes, was finally convinced of his sincerity, and thanked him for his promises of protection. This allowed the rebel lords to claim that Mary had confirmed her acceptance of the deeds, and that she had begged her brother to accept the regency.

In Edinburgh Tolbooth on 22 August 1567, James, Earl of Moray, was proclaimed regent. He made a long acceptance speech in which, with false humility, he expressed his own inadequacy and wished that the office had been conferred on a worthier nobleman, but his scruples were easily overcome, and before the Justice Clerk and others he took the oaths. As regent, he was in effect King of Scotland until James VI reached the age of seventeen. He proceeded to take strenuous measures to establish his government. He made himself master of the castles of Edinburgh and Dunbar and other strongholds. He managed either to win over or silence most of the Queen's Lords, and he inflicted severe punishments on those districts that opposed his appointment.

At a parliament in December Mary's imprisonment and dethroning were declared lawful – not, as had been claimed earlier, because she was determined to be reunited with Bothwell, but on the grounds that conclusive evidence had come to light that she was implicated in Darnley's murder, in

127

the form of certain 'private letters, written wholly with the Queen's own hand'.

While Moray consolidated his regime, Mary remained in close confinement in Loch Leven Castle. Within the space of four months her husband had been murdered, she had been forced into a disagreeable marriage, her kingdom had been taken from her, her child had been crowned in her place, and she had been publicly dishonoured. As if this was not enough, Margaret Erskine, the Lady of Loch Leven, continued to take delight in taunting her prisoner about the ascendancy of Moray, her illegitimate son. Her servants followed her lead, and one in particular, James Drysdale, a bigoted and unprincipled fanatic who had been involved in Rizzio's assassination, hated Mary savagely, at one point declaring that it would give him pleasure to plunge a dagger into her heart. Holding a position of some authority in the household, he probably succeeded in influencing the other domestics, which would hardly have added to Mary's comfort, although she had been allowed to retain a few attendants of her own who proved more than faithful – one or two female and three or four male servants – the most attentive being John Beaton.

However, her personality and her beauty won her two admirers among the younger members of the House of Loch Leven: George Douglas, the youngest son of Lady Douglas, aged about twenty-five, and William Douglas, an orphaned youth of sixteen or seventeen who was a relative of the family and lived in the castle. George in particular was so incensed at the injustice of Mary's plight that he swore not to rest until he had helped her escape, and although William was too young to be of much assistance, he felt just as strongly. George informed Mary's friends in the adjoining districts of his plans, and at his suggestion Lord Seaton travelled in secret to Loch Leven with a fairly large force and laid in wait to help Mary as soon as she was able to find a way to escape across the loch.

They did not have to wait long for her first attempt. Her poor health and low spirits meant that she was in the habit of spending most of the morning in bed, and on 25 March 1568 her laundress entered her room before she was up and took her place in bed while Mary disguised herself in her clothes. With a bundle of laundry in her hand and a muffler over her face, she made her way unsuspected to the boat that was waiting to take the laundress back across the loch. The men in it belonged to the castle but did not realize anything was wrong for some time until one of them noticed that she was anxious to keep her face covered and said teasingly: 'Let us see what kind of a looking damsel this is.' When Mary put up her hands to stop him removing her muffler, it was immediately obvious that they were too soft and white to be a those of a washerwoman. Mary threw aside her disguise, assumed an air of dignity, told the men that she was their queen, and ordered them to row her over to the shore. Although surprised and awe-struck, they refused, but promised that if she would return quietly to the castle they would not inform Sir William Douglas or his mother. News of the incident soon leaked out, however, and George Douglas, together with Beaton and Sempil, two of Mary's servants, were ordered to leave the island and took up residence in the nearby village of Kinross.

Despite the disappointment, neither Mary nor her friends gave up hope. George Douglas was still determined to help, and William remained in the castle, acting with a degree of caution and enterprise beyond his years, which probably prompted the secret delivery of a small picture to Mary portraying a lion being rescued by a mouse.

A second attempt followed a little more than a month later. On Sunday 2 May, around 7 p.m., William Douglas was having supper with the rest of the family. His relative, Sir William, had placed the castle keys beside his plate while he ate, and young William managed to get hold of them, made his way to the door, locked it after him and went to Mary's chamber. He led her through a small postern gate to a boat that had been prepared for her. One of her maids, Jane Kennedy, was a few moments behind them, and as Douglas had locked the postern gate in the mean time, she had to leap from a window but landed safely.

Lord Seaton, James Hamilton of Rochbank and others had been informed of the latest escape attempt by a few words Mary had traced in charcoal on a handkerchief she had managed to send them and were waiting anxiously for the boat's arrival. With Sir William Douglas and his retainers locked up in their own castle, Mary, her maid and her young escort had already set off across the loch. William was not used to rowing, and they made little or no progress until Mary took hold of one of the oars and helped him as best she could.

It was not long before they arrived safely at the opposite shore, where Seaton, Hamilton, Gerge Douglas, Beaton and the rest received Mary joyfully. There was little time for celebration, however. They gave her a horse, surrounded her with a strong guard and galloped all night, arriving at Hamilton the next morning having rested only an hour or two at Lord Seaton's house at Niddry in West Lothian.

Mary never forgot the services of those who rescued her on this occasion. She bestowed pensions on both the Douglases (George was later to become a favourite with her son, James VI), William is mentioned in her last will and testament, and the faithful Beaton did not go unrewarded.

So incredible was the news that Mary had arrived in Hamilton and noblemen and troops were flocking to her from all quarters that Moray, who was holding courts of justice at Glasgow, at first refused to believe it. But if nothing else had convinced him, he might have found the sudden change of attitude even among those he had previously considered his best friends persuasive. Some slipped away, others went in secret to beg Mary's pardon, and quite a few publicly transferred their allegiance to the queen. Moray was advised to join the young king in Stirling but was afraid that leaving Glasgow in a hurry might be interpreted as fleeing, which would have encouraged his enemies and sown doubt among his remaining friends, so he decided to stay and gather his forces as quickly as possible.

Mary did not keep him in suspense regarding her intentions for long. She sent him a message a day or two later, demanding that he surrender his regency and reinstate her. Before the earls, bishops, lords and others who had now gathered round her, she solemnly protested that she had signed the abdication deeds at Loch Leven under duress, and Sir Robert Melville – who had by now left Moray's party for the queen's – vouched for the truth of Mary's words. The abdication was therefore pronounced null and void, and since Moray had issued a proclamation refusing to surrender the regency, both parties prepared for immediate hostilities.

The principal lords who had joined the queen were Argyll, Huntly, Cassils, Rothes, Montrose, Fleming, Livingston, Seaton, Boyd, Herries, Ross, Maxwell, Ogilvy and Oliphant, and her growing party included nine earls, nine bishops, eighteen lords, and many barons and gentlemen. A week later she found herself at the head of an army of six thousand men. Since Hamilton was not a suitable stronghold, they decided to march to Dumbarton Castle, which had long been in the possession of the Hamiltons, and install Mary in safety there until she could assemble a parliament to decide how best to safeguard the country.

When Moray heard on Thursday 13 May that the queen and her troops were en route from Hamilton to Dumbarton and would pass near Glasgow, he decided he had to do everything in his power to head them off – if Mary reached Dumbarton she would be almost invincible and would have time to collect such a strong army that she might be able to chase him out of Scotland again. In any case, Moray was not too worried at the prospect of losing a battle between two armies consisting of only a few thousand men each as he could draw on many more, but as Mary's forces were still relatively small, it might be a fatal blow to her. He assembled his army of some four thousand men on Glasgow Green, and when he received word that the queen was marching along the south side of the Clyde, he crossed the river and met her at the small village of Langside on Cart Water, about two miles south of Glasgow.

Mary was anxious to avoid a battle. She knew that Moray was an excellent tactician and that Kirkcaldy of Grange, the best soldier in Scotland, was with him. However, feelings on both sides were running high, and there was so much ill feeling between the Hamiltons and the Lennoxes in particular that as soon as they came within sight of each other it was obvious that nothing but bloodshed would satisfy them.

The main body of the queen's army was under the command of the Earl of Argyll, the vanguard was led by Claud Hamilton, second son of the Duke of Chatelherault, and the cavalry was under Lord Herries. The Earl of Huntly would have taken a leading role in the battle, but he had set off from Hamilton a few days earlier to collect his followers and had yet to arrive.

Moray himself commanded his main body, Morton led the vanguard, while Kirkcaldy was entrusted with a roving brief, riding about over the whole battlefield and making such alterations in the positions as he felt necessary.

All that stood between the two armies now was a hill, and both were keen to gain possession of it, one side advancing from the east and the other from the west. However, the slope on the side nearest Mary's troops was the steepest, and Kirkcaldy managed to secure the vantage ground for the regent by ordering every mounted man to give a foot-soldier a lift to the top of the hill, where they instantly formed into line. Argyll was therefore forced to take up position on slightly lower ground. Both sides exchanged cannon fire for about half an hour but without much effect.

Eventually, Argyll led his forces forward, determined to take the heights by hand-to-hand combat. The engagement

133

soon spread, Morton, who came down the hill to meet Argyll, driving back the queen's cannoneers and part of her infantry, while Herries led a vigorous charge on Moray's cavalry and routed them. He quickly returned to attack some of the enemy's foot battalions, but as he was advancing directly uphill, he was unable to make much impression on them.

In the mean time, in an attempt to gain more equal ground, Argyll tried to lead his troops round towards the west, and this led to the most desperate phase of the battle. All the forces of both parties were gradually drawn from their previous positions and concentrated on this new ground. For half an hour the outcome was uncertain, but eventually the queen's troops began to waver. The battle was finally decided when reinforcements of two hundred Highlanders arrived for Moray in the nick of time and broke in on Argyll's flank, winning the day. The queen's forces were compelled to retreat, and although Mary's army had lost only about three hundred men, many of her best officers and soldiers were taken prisoner.

Mary had observed the battle with growing alarm from a nearby hill. When she saw the outcome she rode off at full speed with a very small retinue of trusted friends, heading south towards Galloway, where she hoped to be able to escape by land or sea to England or France. They did not stop until they reached Dundrennan Abbey, about two miles from Kirkcudbright and at least sixty from Langside.

She stayed at Dundrennan for two days, holding several discussions with the few friends who had either accompanied her in her flight or joined her afterwards. Herries, her principal adviser, suggested she sail immediately for France, where she had relatives on whom she could depend, even although they might not be able to restore her to her throne, but Mary could not contemplate returning as a fugitive to a country she had left as a queen. Besides, placing herself under the protection of Catholics might offend her subjects and would certainly displease Elizabeth and the English.

Mary was more inclined to place some reliance on the assurances of friendship she had recently received from her sister queen. She was well aware of the hollowness of most of Elizabeth's promises, but this was outweighed by the fear that fleeing to the Continent would mean resigning her crown for ever. After much hesitation she finally decided to go to England and asked Herries to write to Elizabeth's warden at Carlisle to ask for permission to go there. Without waiting for a reply, she rode to the coast with a retinue of eighteen or twenty on Sunday 16 May, boarded a fishing boat and sailed eighteen miles along the coast until she came to the small harbour of Workington in Cumberland. From there she proceeded to the town of Cockermouth, about twenty-six miles from Carlisle. Lord Scroope, the Warden of Carlisle, was in London at this time, but his deputy, Lowther, having sent an express dispatch to Elizabeth informing her of Mary's arrival, assembled the men of rank and influence in the neighbourhood to greet the Scottish queen and conducted her honourably to Carlisle Castle with the assurance that he would protect her from all her enemies until Elizabeth made her decision known.

As soon as the important news reached Elizabeth that Mary was now within her realm – and consequently at her mercy – she saw that she was close to achieving the ultimate

135

aim of all her intrigues. She would have to proceed with caution, however, for she did not yet know either the precise strength of Mary's supporters in Scotland or the degree of interest France might take in her future fate. She therefore immediately despatched Lord Scroope and Sir Francis Knollys, her Vice-Chamberlain, to Carlisle with messages of comfort and condolence. As Mary awaited their arrival, her spirits began to revive, and she was hopeful that Elizabeth would soon express her friendship in deeds as well as words.

CHAPTER

VIII

ELIZABETH VERSUS MARY

If a single generous feeling towards her relative still lurked in Elizabeth's heart, it should have revealed itself now. Mary was no longer a rival queen but an unfortunate woman who had placed herself at the mercy of her nearest neighbour and ally. If it was too much to expect that Elizabeth would supply her with money and arms to enable her to win back her crown, surely she would either allow Mary to seek assistance in France or, if she remained in England, treat her with kindness and hospitality.

When Lord Scroope and Sir Francis Knollys arrived at Carlisle on 29 May 1568, Lord Herries told them that Mary was keen for a personal interview with Elizabeth, but they had been instructed to answer that they were doubtful whether Elizabeth could receive Mary until her innocence of any part in Darnley's murder had been proven. Mary's entourage included Lesley, Bishop of Ross, Lords Herries, Livingston and Fleming, Ladies Livingston and Fleming, Mary Seaton, Lord Seaton's daughter, and other female attendants, George and William Douglas, her two secretaries, Curl and Nawe, and among other servants, Beaton and Sebastian. Claiming that there were too many strangers from

Scotland present, Lord Scroope and Sir Francis Knollys ordered the fortifications of Carlisle Castle to be repaired, and Mary was ordered to stay near the castle.

At her first meeting with Elizabeth's envoys, Mary impressed them both: 'We found her to have an eloquent tongue and a discreet head, and it seems by her doings, that she has stout courage, and a liberal heart adjoined thereto.' When they told her that Elizabeth refused to see her, Mary burst into tears and expressed the bitterest disappointment but quickly composed herself and declared that if she did not receive without delay the aid she had been led to expect, she would immediately demand permission to go on to France, where she was sure she would be granted what Elizabeth denied her. Since she was not allowed to go to London herself, she despatched Herries to look after her interests there. Shortly afterwards, as it was felt unsafe for her to stay so near the border, she allowed herself to be taken to Bolton Castle, a seat of Lord Scroope in the North Riding of Yorkshire.

Meanwhile, Moray was not inactive. He forced the Earl of Huntly, who had collected more than two thousand men and was marching to the queen's assistance when he heard the outcome of the Battle of Langside, to withdraw to the north and disband most of his troops. He scattered the remains of the queen's army which had regrouped under Argyll and Cassilis, and he assembled parliament, which passed Acts of forfeiture and banishment against many of the most powerful lords who had opposed him.

Elizabeth followed his progress with interest and, contrary to the impression she gave Mary, had no desire to stop him. On 8 June she wrote to Moray, addressing him as her 'right trusty, and right well-beloved cousin', and claimed Mary had entrusted her to adjudicate over the differences between Mary and her subjects. She advised him to take steps to make sure he was seen in as favourable a light as possible. Moray had no objection to Elizabeth's role, confident she would ultimately decide in his favour.

Although she had sought her aid, Mary had never dreamt of submitting to Elizabeth's judgment and was indignant when she learned that her rebellious lords were being treated as her equals. She had offered to meet Elizabeth face to face to prove her innocence of all charges, but she had no intention of degrading herself by debating them with her subjects, so she wrote Elizabeth a letter of protest: 'Madam, my good sister, I came into your dominions to ask your assistance, and not to save my life. Scotland and the world have not denounced me. I was conscious of innocence; I was disposed to lay all my transactions before you; and I was willing to do you honour, by making you the restorer of a Queen. But you have afforded me no aid, and no consolation. You even deny me admittance to your presence. I escaped from a prison, and I am again a captive. Can it expose you to censure, to hear the complaints of the unfortunate? You received my bastard brother when he was in open rebellion; I am a Princess, and your equal, and you refuse me this indulgence. Permit me then to leave your dominions. Your severity encourages my enemies, intimidates my friends, and is most cruelly destructive to my interests. You keep me in fetters, and allow my enemies to conquer my realm. I am defenceless; and they enjoy my authority, possess themselves of my revenues, and hold out to me the points of their swords. In the miserable

139

condition to which I am reduced, you invite them to accuse me. Is it too small a misfortune for me to lose my kingdom? Must I, also, be robbed of my integrity and my reputation? Excuse me, if I speak without dissimulation. In your dominions I will not answer to their calumnies and criminations. To you, in a personal conference, I shall at all times be ready to vindicate my conduct; but to sink myself into a level with my rebellious subjects, and to be a party in a suit or trial with them, is an indignity so vile, that I can never submit to it. I can die, but I cannot meet dishonour. Consult, I conjure you, what is right and proper, and entitle yourself to my warmest gratitude; or, if you are inclined not to know me as a sister, and to withhold your kindness, abstain at least from rigour and injustice Be neither my enemy nor my friend; preserve yourself in the coldness of neutrality; and let me be indebted to other princes for my re-establishment in my kingdom.'

Unmoved by this, Elizabeth's treatment of Mary grew even worse, in the hope of intimidating her into complying with her wishes. She kept her under close guard at Bolton to prevent any contact with those who remained loyal to her. She forbade Mary to send Lord Fleming as her ambassador to France and made it plain that Mary could not expect any of her commands to be obeyed unless they met with Elizabeth's approval. The English Privy Council sanctioned all this, holding that until an inquiry had taken place into Mary's conduct, it would be inappropriate to give her the aid she requested. As a result, Mary agreed to nominate commissioners to meet Moray and his own at a conference to state her grievances before commissioners appointed by Elizabeth.

Moray approved of this arrangement because he foresaw the outcome from the beginning. Mary consented to it because she believed that Moray and his accomplices were being summoned solely to answer her complaints. Since she felt her charges were unanswerable, she fondly imagined that she would soon he restored to the power they had usurped.

On 4 October 1568 the conference was opened with much solemnity at York. Mary's commissioners were Lesley, Bishop of Ross, Lords Herries, Livingston and Boyd, Gavin Hamilton, Commendator of Kilwinning, Sir John Gordon of Lochinvar and Sir James Cockburn of Stirling. Moray appointed the Earl of Morton, Bothwell, Bishop of Orkney, Pitcairn, Commendator of Dunfermline, and Lord Lindsay, and MacGill and Balnaves, Buchanan, Secretary Maitland and one or two others were to serve as legal advisers and literary assistants. Elizabeth's commissioners, Thomas Howard, Duke of Norfolk, Thomas Ratcliffe, Earl of Sussex, and Sir Ralph Sadler, were invested with full authority to adjudicate over the issues.

Elizabeth revelled in the situation. Her rival, Mary, heir to an ancient line of monarchs, was her prisoner and was being tried by proxy before Elizabeth's tribunal; the Regent of Scotland, who had the authority of a king, stood in person at the bar, and the fate of a kingdom whose power her ancestors had often dreaded but never been able to subdue permanently was now hers to decide. She had assured Mary that far from allowing her subjects to become her accusers, the conference was to call to account those she accused of criminal acts. However, Elizabeth instructed her commissioners to focus on Moray's complaints against Mary and to assure him privately that even if he had no proof of Mary's guilt, if he could attach sufficient suspicion to her, he and his friends would be allowed to decide the terms under which they would allow Mary to return to Scotland.

Although Mary's commissioners had strong doubts about the impartiality of the court, they felt confident in the justice of their cause, and after declaring that their appearance was not to be construed as implying that Mary had submitted to the English queen, they set out their case. They gave the court a brief account of events since Mary's marriage to Bothwell, including Morton's rebellion, her voluntary surrender at Carberry Hill, her imprisonment at Loch Leven, the forced abdication, the coronation of her infant son and the appointment of Moray as regent, her defeat at Langside, and Moray's undutiful conduct since.

Moray made a lengthy speech in defence, claiming that the Earl of Bothwell's conduct in abducting the queen and subsequently marrying her had convinced the nobility that he was the prime culprit for Darnley's murder. They had taken up arms to see justice done and rescue the queen from Bothwell's clutches, and as soon as she agreed to part from him, they had conducted her to the safety of Edinburgh. When they asked her to agree to punish the murderers and have the marriage dissolved, she had declared her intention to abdicate and leave the country with Bothwell. To keep them apart, they had been forced to take her into custody at Loch Leven for a while. During her stay there, weary of the demands of government and realizing that she was out of favour with her subjects, she had renounced her crown voluntarily in favour of her son and appointed Moray regent.

Everything he had done since had been in accordance with the legal authority she had invested in him and he should be allowed to continue to govern the country on behalf of the infant king in peace.

Mary's commissioners gave a damning rebuttal of Moray's defence. Far from being aware at the time of her marriage that Bothwell was the chief culprit for Darnley's murder, she had witnessed him being acquitted of all suspicion at trial. Most of her ministers had petitioned her to marry Bothwell, and neither before nor after the marriage had any warned her against it or expressed unhappiness with it until they had taken up arms. At Carberry Hill she parted from Bothwell willingly, as they had witnessed, and if he was guilty of the crimes, which she did not believe at the time, they were to blame for allowing him to escape. On being taken to Edinburgh, rather than being honoured as their queen as they had promised, she had been treated as a captive, and far from remaining attached to Bothwell, she had repeatedly asked for an inquiry into all the charges against him. Despite this, she had been taken away under cover of darkness and imprisoned in Loch Leven Castle. While there, she had been forced to sign the deeds of abdication under threats to her life. As a result, the coronation of her son was unlawful and treasonable, and Moray's appointment as regent served to prove that force and deception had been used, for even if she had been willing to abdicate, there were many others she would have preferred to appoint as regent. Therefore, she required the Queen of England to support her in the peaceful government of her realm, and to declare Moray's regency null from the beginning.

Not only were the English commissioners surprised at the weakness of Moray's defence, even he was conscious that he had failed to give plausible reasons for usurping his sister's throne. Elizabeth feared that she would be forced to take measures against her secret ally unless he was able to strengthen his case and press home his charges more forcefully. When she sent a message warning him of this, Moray, Maitland and Buchanan agreed that they would have to fall back on a ploy that they had been keeping in reserve.

Moray had already accused Mary of collaborating in Darnley's assassination, but as he had made the charge soon after his return from France, it was suspected he was just trying to justify keeping her at Loch Leven. No evidence had been produced against her, despite the fact that Moray had in his possession a collection of letters and sonnets alleged to be in Mary's own hand and addressed to Bothwell in which she declared her love for him and her guilt in Darnley's murder. Moray was reluctant to rely on the letters if he could avoid it, and even after he realized they would be needed to bolster his case, he did not want to produce them openly until he had sought the English commissioners' opinion on them.

On 10 October, Maitland, MacGill and Buchanan held a secret meeting with Norfolk, Sussex and Sadler, and laid the mysterious documents before them. They informed Elizabeth about them the next day and asked whether she thought they would be sufficient evidence to convict Mary. As soon as Elizabeth heard about the letters she decided to take charge of the proceedings and moved the conference from York to Westminster, adding the Earls of Arundel and Leicester, Lord Clinton, Sir Nicolas Bacon and Sir William

Cecil to her commissioners, while Mary remained imprisoned at Bolton.

Although Mary at first approved of the new arrangements, she soon realized that they were not intended to further her cause. What galled her most was that although Elizabeth still refused to meet Mary in person, she held an audience with Moray – hardly the act of an impartial umpire. During their audience, Elizabeth informed Moray that if he would accuse Mary of being party to the murder of Darnley and produce the incriminating letters, she would authorize his continuing as regent.

On 26 November, claiming that he had been anxious to avoid bringing infamy on the mother of his gracious king, James VI, but was now forced to disclose certain evidence because it was maintained that his previous defence was inadequate, he presented the English commissioners with a document formally charging Mary with her husband's murder. The same charge had already been made in the Scottish parliament in December 1567 but without producing any evidence. Now, with Mary a prisoner in the hands of her jealous rival, Moray assumed that any inconsistencies in his claims would be overlooked.

Before Mary's commissioners were able to inform her of the unexpected turn of events, fresh instructions from her dated 22 November arrived from Bolton. Mary raised several complaints: first, although she had come to England assured of Elizabeth's friendship, she had taken no steps to restore her to her throne but had kept her prisoner; second, although she had complied with Elizabeth's request that she ask her loyal subjects in Scotland to cease hostilities, Moray had not been prevented from harassing and attacking them, and third, having established that the initial charges against her were groundless, instead of reinstating her the conference had been moved farther away from where she was being held, hindering communication with her commissioners. Finally, they were to proceed no further with the conference until she had been given equal treatment to Moray and allowed to argue her case in person before Elizabeth.

Mary's commissioners told Elizabeth that although they deeply regretted that their countrymen had chosen to level such a shameful charge to obscure their own guilt, they could not continue with the conference in the present circumstances, having begun at York as plaintiffs and now finding themselves defending the accused. Nevertheless, although Moray's conduct was intolerable, they would not withdraw from the conference if Mary was allowed to appear in person. Elizabeth had no intention of agreeing to this request. Her private reason was fear of the truth, but the one she advanced in public was preposterous: 'As to your desire that your Sovereign should come to my presence to declare her innocence in this cause, you will understand, that from the beginning why she was debarred therefrom, was through the bruit and slander that was passed upon her, that she was participant of such a heinous crime as the murder of her husband; and I thought it best for your mistress's weal and honour, and also, for mine own, that trial should be taken thereof before her coming to me; for I could never believe, nor yet will, that ever she did assent thereto.' Faced with a stalemate, Mary's commissioners declared that as far as they were concerned, the conference was closed.

It would not have suited Elizabeth's purpose to leave matters unresolved, so she ordered Moray and his colleagues to be called before the conference to act out a scene she had arranged with them beforehand. She commanded her commissioners to rebuke Moray for accusing Mary of a crime so horrible that if it could be proved true she would be infamous to all the princes of the world. Moray answered that since he had displeased Elizabeth, he was willing to show the commissioners the written evidence that had led him to charge Mary, which would satisfy them that he had not done so without good grounds.

Elizabeth could not have wished for more. With Mary's commissioners out of the way, Moray's evidence could now be presented to the world without fear of contradiction and used to justify her own severity. However, Mary very nearly frustrated her plans. As soon as she heard of this new accusation and the evidence produced to support it, she wrote to her commissioners: 'We have seen the copy which you have sent us of the false and unlawful accusation presented against us by some of our rebels, together with the declarations and protestations made by you thereon before the Queen of England, our good sister's Commissioners, wherein you have obeyed our commands to refuse consenting to any further proceedings, if the presence of our sister were refused us. But that our rebels may see that they have not closed your mouths, you may offer a reply to the pretended excuse and cloak of their wicked actions, falsity and disloyalty, whereof you had no information before, it being a thing so horrible that neither we nor you could have imagined it would have fallen into the thoughts of the said rebels.'

At Mary's instruction, her commissioners rejoined the conference and dismissed the charges as false in every particular and nothing but a device to justify Moray's own 'detestable doings and ambitious purpose'. They demanded that the letters, or at least copies of them, be produced, and declared that Mary would prove that the very men who now accused her of murder were themselves the instigators, and in some cases the executors, of the deed.

Her bluff having been called, Elizabeth refused to allow duplicates of the evidence to be sent to Mary and hurriedly broke up the conference. Although Moray and his allies had been formally accused of sharing in Bothwell's guilt, Moray was allowed to return to his regency, but Mary, who had not been allowed to defend herself against similar charges, was kept in even closer captivity than ever. Although she continued to petition to see the writings, Elizabeth refused to surrender them except on conditions that were unacceptable to Mary's commissioners.

As Mary had not been found guilty of any crime and Moray had been allowed to go home, Mary asked for leave either to return to Scotland or go to France. Elizabeth refused but promised that if she would give up her claim to the crown in favour of her son, she would be allowed to remain in England as a guest. Mary rejected the proposal with scorn, saying: 'The eyes of all Europe are upon me at this moment and were I thus tamely to yield to my adversaries, I should be pronouncing my own condemnation. A thousand times rather would I submit to death than inflict this stain upon my honour. The last words I speak shall be those of the Queen of Scotland.'

CHAPTER

IX

*D*ETENTION WITHOUT TRIAL

Moray and his commissioners returned home on 12 January 1569 with a loan of £5,000 from Elizabeth 'for the maintenance of peace between the realms of England and Scotland' – in other words, as a bribe to secure his future co-operation. Elizabeth was reluctant to allow Mary to remain in one place for long in case she formed connections and friendships that might allow her to escape, so she moved her from Bolton and placed her in the charge of Lord Shrewsbury at Tutbury Castle in Staffordshire.

Lord Shrewsbury did not treat her badly, taking her on occasional visits to several mansions he possessed in different parts of England, but wherever she went she was very strictly guarded. One of Cecil's friends, in a letter he wrote to him about this time, gives an insight into how she passed the days: 'If I might give advice, there should very few subjects of this land have access to a conference with this lady; for, beside that she is a goodly personage (and yet in truth not comparable to our Sovereign), she hath withal an alluring grace, a pretty Scotch speech, and a searching wit, clouded with mildness. . . . Lord Shrewsbury is very watchful of his charge;

but the Queen overwatches them all, for it is one of the clock at least every night ere she go to bed. I asked her grace, since the weather did cut off all exercise abroad, how she passed the time within? She said, that all the day she wrought with her needle, and that the diversity of the colours made the work seem less tedious; and she continued so long till even pain made her give over; and with that laid her hand upon her left side, and complained of an old grief newly increased there. She then entered upon a pretty disputable comparison between carving, painting, and working with the needle, affirming painting, in her own opinion, for the most commendable quality.'

Mary, at this point aged twenty-seven, may have seemed outwardly resigned to captivity, but the injustice of her imprisonment never ceased to prey on her mind. Elizabeth and Cecil had tried to justify keeping her prisoner on four grounds: first, that she was a lawful prisoner under good treaties, but they did not specify which treaties they were referring to; second, that they could not free her until she had made amends for the wrong she had done Elizabeth by openly claiming the crown of England, but Mary had made the claim when married to Francis and expressly relinquished it on his death; third, that Elizabeth possessed superiority over the crown of Scotland, but this antiquated notion, arising from the subservience of John Balliol to Edward I in 1292, had long been relinquished and had never been acknowledged in any treaty between the two nations; fourth, that Elizabeth was bound to attend to the petition of her subjects 'in matters of blood', but although Lord and Lady Lennox had presented a petition against Mary, since Mary was not one of her subjects Elizabeth had no power either to grant or refuse such a petition.

Although Mary's enemies seemed to have won, her friends refused to give up. Moray presided over a divided kingdom, and only after a protracted and disastrous civil war was he able to overcome the hostility of Chatelherault, Argyll, Huntly and others. In England, the Duke of Norfolk – Elizabeth's principal commissioner at the conference and one of her most powerful lords – was scheming more actively than ever. When Mary arrived in England he had plotted to take the Scottish throne by marrying her. Far from being alarmed by the accusations against her, he openly expressed his conviction that they were false and persuaded a number of the English nobility to do all they could to help him court her. Although it seems he was unable to meet her in person, many letters passed between them. She soon saw that her best chance of being restored to power lay in joining her interests with those of Norfolk, and she promised that despite her unfortunate experience of matrimony, she would marry him as soon as he helped her regain her liberty. Elizabeth eventually discovered Norfolk's plans, however, and sent him to the Tower of London, where he was kept under close arrest for more than nine months, while the Earls of Arundel, Pembroke and Leicester, who had supported him, fell into disgrace. Mary was watched even more closely than before, and Hastings, Earl of Huntingdon, was appointed to superintend her imprisonment with Shrewsbury.

Norfolk had not been in the Tower for long when an open rebellion broke out in the northern counties, headed by the Earls of Northumberland and Westmoreland. Although there is no reason to believe that Mary gave it any encouragement, the declaration published by the earls gave one of their grounds for complaint as the lack of a law for settling the succession. They marched towards Tutbury with the intention of freeing Mary, and they might have succeeded had she not been hurriedly moved to Coventry. Elizabeth sent an army against the rebels, and they were quickly dispersed. Westmoreland went into hiding in the Borders, but Northumberland, proceeding farther into Scotland, was seized by Moray and confined in Loch Leven Castle – probably in the very apartments Mary had occupied.

An event at the beginning of 1570 changed the situation radically and aroused mixed feelings in Mary. Realizing the danger of continuing to detain such an important prisoner, Elizabeth had just begun negotiations with Moray to return his sister to him when she received the unexpected and unwelcome news that he had been assassinated at Linlithgow in an act of revenge by James Hamilton of Bothwellhaugh.

His treatment of his sister had been inexcusable and nearly murderous, but Mary's tears when she heard of his untimely death reflect the fact that Moray was a complex character. He was a patron of literature and attentive to his friends, because patronage and a large number of friends confer power. He was cold but not often cruel, because he saw it was usually in his own interest to be humane. He had far too much ambition to be an upright man and far too much good sense to be an undisguised villain. In short, he was so used to hiding his real intentions and feelings that he was probably not aware himself when he was acting from good motives and when from bad ones.

The Earl of Lennox was appointed the new regent, while Elizabeth continued in her efforts to divide Scotland. She pretended to enter into new negotiations with Mary, as she did from time to time when pressed by Mary's more powerful friends, but although commissioners were appointed to meet with Morton, nothing was resolved.

Around this time, Elizabeth was particularly annoyed when Pope Pius V excommunicated her, assuming wrongly that Mary had been involved in the decision, and when a man named Felton fixed a copy of the papal bull on the gate of the Bishop of London's palace, she had him executed. In her anger, she ordered that Mary should not be allowed outside and she did not revoke this order until it was made apparent to her that Mary's health was suffering badly. The pain in her left side had grown much worse recently, and she had been advised to take baths in white wine as a tonic.

Later in the year she was moved from Tutbury, first to Chatsworth and then to the Earl of Shrewsbury's castle at Sheffield. Among her thirty or so attendants were Lord and Lady Livingston, her young friend William Douglas, Castel, her French physician, and Roulet, her French Secretary. Roulet's death while she was at Sheffield caused her much grief. All communication with her distant friends was denied her, her letters were continually intercepted and copies of the originals sent to Cecil, but she was too proud to complain, and when she wrote to inquire after her faithful servant the Bishop of Ross, whom Elizabeth had imprisoned because of his efforts on Mary's behalf, all she allowed herself to say was that she pitied poor prisoners, for she was treated like one herself.

In 1571, the Duke of Norfolk, by this time released from

the Tower, unwisely resumed his campaign to release Mary and marry her, and the secret correspondence between them was renewed. Norfolk was impatient to press forward with his plans, even willing to risk treason. With the Spanish ambassador and Rodolphi, a Florentine merchant residing in London who was an agent of the court of Rome, he entered into a conspiracy that would have brought down the government if it had succeeded.

The plan was that the Duke of Alva should land in England with a large army, and be joined immediately by Norfolk and his friends. They were then to proclaim Mary's right to the English throne, call on all good Catholics to support them and march to London. The pope and the King of Spain readily agreed to the scheme, and everything appeared to be going according to plan when one of Norfolk's servants revealed the plot to Elizabeth. Norfolk was immediately arrested, thrown into prison, tried for high treason, found guilty and condemned to death. Elizabeth gave a show of reluctance to sign Norfolk's death warrant, since he had rendered her good services in the past, but was eventually able to bring herself to consign him to the scaffold. There he confessed that he had been justly found guilty of corresponding with the Queen of Scots without the knowledge of his own queen. He died as he had lived, with undaunted courage. When the executioner offered him a napkin to cover his eyes, he refused it, saying: 'I fear not death.' Laying his head on the block, it was taken off with one blow.

Elizabeth, eager to implicate Mary in Norfolk's guilt, sent commissioners to confront her with her offences. Mary heard all they had to say with the utmost calmness, then replied that although she was a queen in her own right and did not consider herself accountable either to them or their mistress, she had no hesitation in assuring them of the injustice of their accusations. She protested that she had never intended any harm to Elizabeth by planning to marry Norfolk, and that she had neither encouraged him to raise a rebellion nor been privy to it – on the contrary, she would reveal any conspiracy against the Queen of England that came to her attention. Although Rodolphi had been of use to her in sending letters abroad, she had never received any from him. As to attempting to escape, she willingly listened to anyone who offered to help her and had corresponded with several of them in cipher, but far from having any hand in the bull of excommunication, when a copy of it was sent to her she had burned it after reading it, and she had had no communication with any foreign state about anything except her restoration to her own kingdom. Satisfied with her reply, the commissioners returned to London.

Meanwhile, Scotland was suffering the miseries of civil war. The Earl of Lennox was a feeble and incompetent successor to Moray, and seeing that he was unable to maintain his authority and that the tide of public opinion against the unjust imprisonment of Mary was growing stronger, many of those who had stood by Moray deserted to the opposite faction, including Secretary Maitland and Kirkcaldy of Grange. Both factions were evenly matched, raising armies, convening parliaments, fighting battles, besieging towns and ordering executions, and neighbours, friends and relatives found themselves on opposing sides as 'Kingsmen' or 'Queensmen' as political hatred mingled with religious zeal.

155

One of Lennox's major successes was taking Dumbarton Castle from the Queen's Lords, the Archbishop of St Andrews being executed without trial. No bishop had ever been treated like this in Scotland before, and while the king's adherents were glad to be rid of a zealous opponent, it inflamed the Queen's Lords to such an extent that their watchword became: 'Think on the Archbishop of St Andrews!' Lennox was to pay dearly for this act. When Kirkcaldy succeeded in taking the town of Stirling in a surprise attack, Lennox surrendered but was shot on the orders of Lord Claud Hamilton, the deceased archbishop's brother. The Earl of Mar was elected regent in his place.

In 1572, the massacre of the Huguenots in France was a severe setback to Mary's cause, angering Protestants throughout Europe and arousing fury at the mere mention of a Catholic sovereign's name. Although Mary herself had always advocated religious tolerance, her connection with the perpetrators of the outrage, Charles IX of France and Catherine de Medici, allowed her enemies to ensure that she shared in the blame. Elizabeth promoted the circulation of Buchanan's notorious *Ane Detectioun of the doinges of Marie quene of Scottes*, which had been published a short time earlier. She ordered Cecil to send a number of copies to Walsingham, her ambassador in Paris, to be presented to the king and leading persons in the French court to attempt to disgrace her. On the other hand, Bishop Lesley's *Defence of Queen Mary's Honour* was banned and Lesley had to have it published abroad.

In Scotland, too, Mary's support was gradually dwindling as the hopelessness of her cause became apparent. Mar might have achieved a general peace had not Morton's superior influence and persistent cruelty drawn the civil war out. Finding himself thwarted in every peace proposal he advanced, Mar fell into a deep depression that ended in his death before he had been in office a year. Morton succeeded him without opposition and immediately took very violent measures against the queen's friends, who were now divided into two parties, one headed by Chatelherault and Huntly, and the other by Maitland and Kirkcaldy. After some victories over both, he made peace with Chatelherault and Huntly's faction, and having surrounded Edinburgh Castle on all sides in conjunction with some troops Elizabeth had sent to assist him, he finally forced Maitland and Kirkcaldy to surrender. Kirkcaldy of Grange, the bravest and most honest man in Scotland, was hanged at Edinburgh Cross, and Secretary Maitland avoided a similar fate only by committing suicide.

About the same time, John Knox died at the age of sixty-seven. A rough, unpolished, courageous man of integrity, his many failings may be attributed more to the times he lived in than any fault of his own, and his violence, acrimony and strong prejudices were the instruments he chose to advance the Reformation.

In 1573, Mary's ill health led her to request to be moved from Sheffield to the wells at Buxton. She had been badly affected by the news she had recently received from Scotland and the apparent annihilation of all her hopes. At Buxton, which was then the most fashionable watering place in England, she was obliged to live in complete seclusion, and the waters could be of little benefit to her without the aid of fresh air, exercise and amusement. The faithful Lesley, although detained at a distance, did all he could to console her, and wrote two treatises, for her, '*Piæ afflicti animi meditationes divinaque remedia*' and '*Tranquillitatis animi conservatio et munimentum*'. She was so pleased with many parts of the first in particular that she occupied herself paraphrasing them into French verse. Soon afterwards, Elizabeth allowed Lesley to go to France, where he continued to lobby for his mistress, visiting several foreign courts and suffering many inconveniences and hardships, dying at a good old age the next year.

In 1574, Mary suffered more misfortune when her brother-in-law, Charles IX, died. He was succeeded by the Duke of Anjou, who took the title of Henry III and had little inclination to help Mary because of his long enmity with the House of Guise. But an even worse blow was the death of her uncle, the Cardinal of Lorraine, who had always supported her and been her confidant in her greatest troubles.

Satisfied with keeping her rival securely imprisoned, Elizabeth now busied herself with other political affairs, and in Scotland, as James VI grew up and the years passed, death or other causes gradually diminished Mary's followers. Although the country was far from peaceful, even those who opposed the Earl of Morton's regency found it more profitable to associate themselves with the young king than the absent queen. Mary gradually became more solitary and more depressed. Although still in the prime of life, she had seen almost all her best friends – and some of her worst enemies – die before her.

But Elizabeth had no sympathy for her grief, and every rumour she heard only served as an excuse for imposing more restrictions on Mary. Deprived even of the few female friends who at first were allowed to attend her, allowed no visitors, rarely permitted to hunt or hawk or take any exercise out of doors, spending her days in wearisome monotony, no wonder her health and her spirits broke down.

She wrote from Tutbury in 1580: 'To convey to you an idea of my present situation, I am on all sides enclosed by fortified walls, on the summit of a hill which lies exposed to every wind of heaven: within these bounds, not unlike the wood of Vincennes, is a very old edifice, originally a hunting lodge, built merely of lath and plaster, the plaster in many places crumbling away. This edifice, detached from the walls about twenty feet, is sunk so low, that the rampart of earth behind the wall is level with the highest part of the building, so that here the sun can never penetrate, neither does any pure air ever visit this habitation, on which descend drizzling damps and eternal fogs, to such excess, that not an article of furniture can be placed beneath the roof, but in four days it becomes covered with green mould. I leave you to judge in what manner such humidity must act upon the human frame . . . the apartments are in general more like dungeons prepared for the reception of the vilest criminals . . . I have for my own person but two miserable little chambers, so intensely cold during the night, that but for ramparts and entrenchments of tapestry and curtains, it would be impossible to prolong my existence; and of those who have sat up with me during my illness, not one has escaped malady. Sir Amias can testify that three of my women have been rendered ill by this severe temperature, and even my physician declines taking charge of my health the ensuing winter, unless I shall be permitted to change my habitation. . . . for taking air and exercise, either on foot or in my chair, I have but about a quarter of an acre behind the stables, round which Somers last year planted a quickset hedge, a spot more proper for swine than to be cultivated as a garden. . . . As it was here that I first began to be treated with rigour and indignity, I have conceived, from that time, this mansion to be singularly unlucky to me, and in this sinister impression I have been confirmed by the tragical catastrophe of the poor priest of whom I wrote to you, who, having been tortured for his religion, was at length found hanging in front of my window.'

In 1581, Mary described in detail the deterioration in her condition: 'I am reduced to such an excessive weakness, especially in my legs, that I am not able to walk a hundred steps, and yet I am at this moment better than I have been for these six months past. Ever since last Easter, I have been obliged to make my servants carry me in a chair; and you may judge how seldom I am thus transported from one spot to another, when there are so few people about me fit for such an employment.' Only her inner resources kept her going, attending to her religious duties with the strictest care and devoting much of her time to reading and writing.

But the most celebrated of all Mary's efforts during her captivity is a long and eloquent letter addressed to Elizabeth in 1582, when she heard that her son had been seized during a raid on Ruthven: 'I am no longer able to resist laying my heart before you; and while I desire that my just complaints shall be engraved in your conscience, it is my hope that they will also descend to posterity, to prove the misery into which I have been brought by the injustice and cruelty of my enemies. Having in vain looked to you for support against their various devices, I shall now carry my appeal to the Eternal

God, the Judge of both, whose dominion is over all the princes of the earth. I shall appeal to Him to arbitrate between us; and would request you, Madam, to remember, that in His sight nothing can be disguised by the paint and artifices of the world.'

Then, after recounting the wrongs Elizabeth had done her ever since she became Queen of Scots, she continues: 'To take away every foundation of dispute and misunderstand between us, I invite you, Madam, to examine into every report against me, and to grant to every person the liberty of accusing me publicly; and while I freely solicit you to take every advantage to my prejudice, I only request that you will not condemn me without a hearing. If it be proved that I have done evil, let me suffer for it; if I am guiltless, do not take upon yourself the responsibility, before God and man, of punishing me unjustly. Let not my enemies be afraid that I aim any longer at dispossessing them of their usurped authority. I look now to no other kingdom but that of Heaven, and would wish to prepare myself for it, knowing that my sorrows will never cease till I arrive there.'

She then speaks of her son and begs Elizabeth to intervene on his behalf, concluding: 'I am very weak and helpless, and do beseech you to give me some solitary mark of your friendship. Bind your own relations to yourself; let me have the happiness of knowing, before I die, that a reconciliation has taken place between us, and that, when my soul quits my body, it will not be necessary for it to carry complaints of your injustice to the throne of my creator.'

In response, Elizabeth sent Beal, the Clerk of her Privy Council, to rebuke Mary for complaining too much.

Meanwhile in Scotland, Morton's intolerable tyranny having turned most of the nobility against him and the young king having nearly arrived at an age when he could act and think for himself, the regent was forced very unwillingly to retire from office. Even then he continued to plot, and it was rumoured that he intended seizing the king and taking him captive to England. Whether there was any truth in this report or not, James was anxious to get rid of him, and the best way seemed to be to accuse Morton of sharing in Bothwell's guilt.

His trial does not seem to have been conducted with any particular regard to justice, but he was allowed a jury of his peers who found him guilty of having been party to or aware of the conspiracy against the late king, of concealing it and of being 'art and part' in the murder. Morton confessed that he had known of the intended murder and had concealed it, but absolutely denied having been 'art and part' in it. Nevertheless, on 1 June 1581 he was condemned to death. He had recently introduced an instrument of execution, similar to a guillotine, called the maiden, and the next day he was its first victim. His head was displayed on the public prison in Edinburgh, and his body was buried privately by a few servants.

CHAPTER X

THE FINAL ACT

Debilitated and deprived of both wealth and power as Mary had been, even after sixteen years in confinement her name continued to be a watchword not only to her remaining friends throughout Christendom but anyone who wanted to stir up civil unrest in England for whatever reason. Her sufferings and cruel treatment were used as an excuse for many plots with anti-constitutional aims, but although Mary openly declared that the injustice of her captivity entitled her to use any means to free herself, she acted only in self-defence and would not sanction any criminal acts. However, if a nobleman of influence like Norfolk or a man of integrity like Lesley wanted to arrange a scheme for her release, she was always willing to go along with their proposals.

Elizabeth must have thought these inconveniences a price worth paying for the pleasure of seeing the Queen of Scots a helpless hostage in her hands, but in 1585 a number of her nobility formed an association sanctioned by parliament and sworn to defend Elizabeth against all her enemies. Alarmed by a recent attempt by a fanatical Roman Catholic to assassinate the queen because she had been excommunicated by the pope, parliament also passed an Act that stipulated: 'That if any rebellion should be excited in the kingdom, or anything attempted to the hurt of her Majesty's person, by or for any person pretending a title to the crown, the Queen should empower twenty-four persons, by a commission under the Great Seal, to examine into and pass sentence upon such offences; and that, after judgment given, a proclamation should be issued, declaring the persons whom they found guilty excluded from any right to the crown; and her Majesty's subjects might lawfully pursue every one of them to the death; and that, if any design against the life of the Queen took effect, the persons by or for whom such a detestable act was executed, and their issues, being in any wise assenting or privy to the same, should be disabled for ever from pretending to the crown, and be pursued to death, in the like manner.'

Under the terms of this questionable Act, Mary could be held accountable for practically any of the numerous plots against Elizabeth, and it was not long before parliament had an opportunity to apply it.

In 1586, three English priests who had been educated at Rheims developed the belief that Pope Pius V's excommunication of Elizabeth had been divinely inspired and began a conspiracy against her. They sent an officer named Savage and another priest named Ballard to England to contact those they thought might serve as allies and began negotiations with the Spanish ambassador in Paris. He promised assistance, but only if they mustered strong support in England and removed Elizabeth from the throne.

Anthony Babington, a landed gentleman from Derbyshire, had spent some time in France, where the Archbishop of

Glasgow's extravagant praise of Mary inspired him to find some means to win her gratitude and esteem, so he introduced Savage and Ballard to a number of respectable Roman Catholics. They began a secret correspondence with Mary via her secretaries, Nawe and Curl. Now under the strict custody of Sir Amias Paulet and Sir Drue Drury in Chartley Castle in Staffordshire, Mary found it difficult to correspond with her friends at all, and the conspirators had to bribe one of the servants to smuggle the letters in and out. Mary did not offer them much encouragement. Not only had she almost given up hope of ever being freed, she realized that the recent Act meant that she would be held responsible for the whole plot, but she probably authorized her secretaries to reply to Babington and his associates once or twice.

Everything seemed to be proceeding smoothly and all the necessary arrangements were in place. Some of the conspirators were to instigate a rebellion in several parts of the kingdom at once; Savage, Ballard and four others took solemn oaths to assassinate Elizabeth; Babington himself undertook to lead a party to rescue Mary, and they could expect foreign assistance once the insurrection was under way. However, their organization had been infiltrated by a man called Polly who was sent to spy on them by Elizabeth's minister Walsingham.

To be certain of securing evidence of their guilt, Walsingham allowed Savage, Ballard and the other four would-be assassins to remain under observation in London while they waited for their chance to strike, but Elizabeth felt this was tempting fate and insisted on having them arrested. Ballard was captured, but his accomplices fled from London and went into hiding in the country, disguising their appearance and doing all they could to avoid detection. However, after a few days they were discovered and taken to London, where public feeling against them was so strong that the city bells were rung and bonfires were lit. Walsingham managed to arrest all the other conspirators scattered throughout the kingdom within a short time, and fourteen of the principal conspirators were immediately tried, condemned and executed.

But the death of these men was not enough for Elizabeth. Mary's cause had lent this conspiracy a degree of respectability, so she was regarded as the chief culprit. Walsingham knew that Mary's secretaries and the conspirators had been in communication, and before Mary had heard that Babington's plot had been discovered, he sent Sir Thomas Gorges to Chartley to confront her and to try to find additional grounds for suspicion. Sir Thomas arrived just as she was about to embark on a carriage ride. Without allowing her to alight, he abruptly told her of Babington's fate. Entering the castle, he had Nawe and Curl taken into custody, broke into Mary's private cabinets, seized all her letters and papers, and sent them off to Elizabeth immediately. He also took possession of all her money, 'lest she should use it for corruption'. She was not allowed to return to Chartley for some days but was moved from one castle to another. When she was finally brought back and saw how she had been robbed in her absence she wept bitterly, but in the midst of her tears said: 'There are two things, however, which they cannot take away – my birth and my religion.'

The uproar throughout the nation and her subjects' fears for the safety of their queen meant that Elizabeth could now take measures against Mary that she had until now only been able to dream of. She claimed that not only her own life but the religion and peace of the country were at stake and that unless the Queen of Scots was removed, the whole realm would be lost, but she had difficulty bringing some of her ministers round to her point of view. Many were convinced that Mary had neither instigated nor encouraged Babington's plot and argued that since her state of health meant she was unlikely to live long in any case, it would be better to leave her alone. Nevertheless, Elizabeth and Walsingham finally managed to silence any opposition, and it was decided to prosecute Mary. To give as much dignity and as great a semblance of justice as possible to the proceedings, forty of the most illustrious men in the kingdom were appointed commissioners and placed in charge of hearing the case and deciding the penalty.

On 25 September 1586 Mary was taken from Chartley to Fotheringay Castle in Northamptonshire, where she was more strictly watched than ever by Sir Amias Paulet, who was a harsh and inflexible gaoler. The great hall of the castle was fitted out as a court room, and Elizabeth's commissioners arrived on 11 October. They would have proceeded with the trial immediately, but Mary refused to acknowledge their jurisdiction, claiming they had no right either to arraign or try her: 'I am no subject to Elizabeth, but an independent Queen as well as she; and I will consent to nothing unbecoming the majesty of a crowned head. Worn out as my body is, my mind is not yet so enfeebled as to make me forget what is due to myself, my ancestors, and my country. Whatever the laws of England may be, I am not subject to them;

for I came into the realm only to ask assistance from a sister Queen, and I have been detained an unwilling prisoner.'

For two days the commissioners tried in vain to persuade Mary to appear before them, but since her arguments were irrefutable, they were eventually driven to making threats. They told her they would proceed with the trial whether she consented to be present or not, and that although they were anxious to hear her testimony, if she refused to defend herself they would conclude that she was guilty and pronounce judgment accordingly. Mary would have been well advised to stand her ground, but because she was unwilling to arouse suspicion by refusing the opportunity to establish her innocence she finally gave in, while solemnly protesting that she did not, and never would, acknowledge that Elizabeth had any authority over her.

The trial began on 14 October. The upper half of the great hall of Fotheringay Castle had been divided off by a railing, and a chair under a canopy of state was set at one end to represent Elizabeth. Lord Chancellor Bromley, Lord Treasurer Burleigh, fourteen earls, thirteen barons and knights, and members of the Privy Council sat on benches on either side of the room, and the Lord Chief Justice, several doctors of civil law, Popham, the Queen's Attorney, her solicitors, sergeants and notaries were seated at a table in the centre. Mary, who was to conduct her own defence, sat in a chair without a canopy at the foot of this table, immediately opposite the chair of state, and observers were allowed to watch proceedings from the other side of the railing.

Popham opened the proceedings by referring to the Act that made it a capital offence to be the person for whom any attempt to assassinate the queen was undertaken. He then described the conspiracy and tried to establish that Mary was implicated in it by producing copies of letters he alleged had passed between her and Babington and several of his accomplices, and statements and confessions that had been extracted from her secretaries. Asserting that the prosecution's case had been made, he wound up his speech with a laboured display of legal knowledge and forensic oratory.

Mary was now called to defend herself, which she did with great composure and dignity. She denied any connection with Babington's conspiracy. Even although the letters he had addressed to her might be genuine, it had not been proven that she ever received them, and her own letters had either been misrepresented or fabricated. As for her secretaries' confessions, they had been made under duress and were therefore inadmissible. Even if any part of them were true, their testimony was worthless since it contravened their oath of fidelity to her, and if they were willing to perjure themselves in one instance, they could not be trusted in another. Besides, a law enacted in the thirteenth year of Elizabeth's reign held that no one could be arraigned for intending to kill the sovereign unless the evidence was presented face to face under oath by two lawful witnesses, and this stipulation had not been complied with.

Even if she agreed to accept the authenticity of many of the papers produced against her, they did not prove her guilty of any crime. After nineteen years' unjust captivity, which had cost her her youth, her health and her happiness, she was surely entitled to make one last effort to regain her liberty, but she strongly objected to the accusation of scheming against the queen, her sister: 'I would disdain to purchase all that is most valuable on earth by the assassination of the meanest of the human race; and worn out, as I now am, with cares and sufferings, the prospect of a crown is not so inviting that I should ruin my soul in order to obtain it. . . . If ever I have given consent by my words, or even by my thoughts, to any attempt against the life of the Queen of England, far from declining the judgment of men, I shall not even pray for the mercy of God.'

Elizabeth's advocates, who had expected an easy victory over someone unfamiliar with legal procedures, were taken aback by Mary's eloquent and skilful defence and were forced to drag the proceedings out for two whole days in the hope of proving their case. Even then, the commissioners did not venture to pronounce judgment, adjourning the court to the Star Chamber at Westminster, where Mary's absence would mean they would face no opposition. The court reconvened on 25 October, and having again examined the unreliable Nawe and Curl, who confirmed their former declarations, passed the unanimous judgment: 'Mary, commonly called Queen of Scots and dowager of France, was accessory to Babington's conspiracy, and had compassed and imagined divers matters within the realm of England, tending to the hurt, death, and destruction of the royal person of Elizabeth, in opposition to the statute framed for her protection.'

Elizabeth ordered this verdict to be laid before parliament when it assembled a few days later. At Walsingham's instigation, its legality was confirmed and the Lord Chancellor was sent with an address to the queen. It stated that her security would be in danger as long as Mary was alive and requested that she order her to be executed immediately. Although Elizabeth no doubt received this advice with great satisfaction, she pretended to be reluctant. She declared that if she were not afraid for the welfare of her people she would freely pardon Mary for all her treasonable practices, and she begged parliament to suggest a less severe sentence. As she expected, this plea for leniency was rejected, and in the pedantic language of the day her ministers reminded her of God's vengeance on Saul for sparing Agag and on Ahab for sparing Benhadad.

Although anxious to be rid of Mary, Elizabeth asked parliament to be content for now 'with an answer without an answer. . . . If I should say, that I will not do what you request, I might say perhaps more than I intend; and if I should say I will do it, I might plunge myself into as much inconvenience as you endeavour to preserve me from.' As well as wishing to appear sensitive and humane to her own subjects, Elizabeth was concerned not to offend foreign courts, so her indecision was probably not all sham. She ordered the sentence against Mary to be published throughout the kingdom and abroad, and waited anxiously for the reaction. As it happened, she had little cause for concern.

Henry III of France had never been more than a very lukewarm advocate for the Queen of Scots, and his occasional protestations on her behalf were mostly for the sake of appearances. The present threat to his cousin's life seems to have concerned him enough to order his ambassador to protest against the sentence in the strongest terms possible, but Elizabeth knew his rage would soon evaporate.

In Scotland, the young King James was surrounded by

ministers who had sold themselves to England, and Elizabeth was well aware that although he might bark, he would not dare to bite. Besides, every effort had been made to turn him against his mother from his earliest years, and since his prospects of succession to the English crown depended on Elizabeth's friendship, he would have no wish to cross her. She was right.

He sent the Master of Gray and Sir Robert Melville as his ambassadors to London to protest 'that it cannot stand with his honour to be a consenter to take his mother's life, but he does not care how strictly she be kept; and is content that all her old knavish servants should be hanged'. Melville acted faithfully, but Gray, wishing to curry favour with Elizabeth, assured her that she had no reason to fear James's resentment since he was indecisive and timid, and whatever might happen, he had no wish to embroil himself in a disastrous war with England. Elizabeth listened to him with satisfaction and instructed Walsingham to inform James that Mary's fate had already been decided by parliament, and it was not within her power to save her. When James received this message, instead of leading an army into the heart of England to rescue his mother, he simply informed his subjects and ordered prayers to be said for her in all the nation's churches, 'that it might please God to enlighten her with the light of his truth, and to protect her from the danger which was hanging over her'.

When messengers announced to Mary that she had been sentenced to death, far from receiving the news with dismay, she solemnly raised her hands to heaven and thanked God that she would soon be free of her troubles. There were more in store, however. Her keepers, Sir Amias Paulet and Sir Drue Drury, were no longer willing to treat her with the reverence and respect due her rank and sex. The canopy of state, which she had always ordered to be erected in her apartment wherever she went, was taken down, and every badge of royalty was removed. She was informed that she was no longer to be regarded as a princess, but as a criminal, and those who came into her presence stood before her without uncovering their heads or paying obeisance. She was refused a Catholic priest, and instead an Episcopalian bishop was sent to point out and correct the errors of her ways. But Mary managed to rise above all these indignities: 'In despite of your Sovereign and her subservient judges, I will die a Queen. My royal character is indelible, and I will surrender it with my spirit to the Almighty God, from whom I received it, and to whom my honour and my innocence are fully known.'

Her final letter to Elizabeth in December 1586 reveals her strength of character: 'Madam, I thank God from the bottom of my heart, that, by the sentence which has been passed against me, he is about to put an end to my tedious pilgrimage. I would not wish it prolonged, though it were in my power, having had enough of time to experience its bitterness. I write at present only to make three last requests which, as I can expect no favour from your implacable ministers, I should wish to owe to your Majesty, and to no other. First, as in England, I cannot hope to be buried according to the solemnities of the Catholic Church (the religion of the ancient Kings, your ancestors and mine, being now changed), and as in Scotland they have already violated the

173

ashes of my progenitors, I have to request, that, as soon as my enemies have bathed their hands in my innocent blood, my domestics may be allowed to inter my body in some consecrated ground; and, above all, that they may be permitted to carry it to France, where the bones of the Queen, my most honoured mother, repose. Thus, that poor frame, which has never enjoyed repose so long as it has been joined to my soul, may find it at last when they will be separated. Second, as I dread the tyranny of the harsh men, to whose power you have abandoned me, I entreat your Majesty that I may not be executed in secret, but in the presence of my servants and other persons, who may bear testimony of my faith and fidelity to the true church, and guard the last hours of my life, and my last sighs from the false rumours which my adversaries may spread abroad. Third, I request that my domestics, who have served me through so much misery, and with so much constancy, may be allowed to retire without molestation wherever they choose, to enjoy for the remainder of their lives the small legacies which my poverty has enabled me to bequeath to them. I conjure you, Madam, by the blood of Jesus Christ, by our consanguinity, by the memory of Henry VII, our common father, and by the royal title which I carry with me to death, not to refuse me those reasonable demands, but to assure me, by a letter under your own hand, that you will comply with them; and I shall then die as I have lived, your affectionate sister and prisoner, Mary, Queen of Scots.'

No reply from Elizabeth has ever come to light, but letters from her to Sir Amias Paulet show that she was so reluctant to take responsibility for Mary's death that she even asked him to have her assassinated. Although Paulet was a harsh and violent man, he refused. Finally realizing she had no alternative, she ordered her secretary, Davidson, to bring her the warrant for Mary's execution, read it carefully, then signed it. She told Davidson to take it to Walsingham, saying with a smile that she was afraid he would die of grief when he saw it. Walsingham passed it to the Chancellor, who affixed the Great Seal and commissioned the Earls of Shrewsbury, Kent and Derby and others to carry it out. To complete the solemn farce, Elizabeth then pretended that Davidson had obeyed her orders too quickly and sentenced him to life imprisonment.

On 7 February 1587 the earls who had been commissioned to superintend the execution arrived at Fotheringay. After dining together, they sent word to Mary that they wished to speak to her. She was ill in bed, but when she was told it was an urgent matter she got up and received them in her own chamber, attended by her six maidservants, her physician, her surgeon, her apothecary and four or five male servants. The Earl of Shrewsbury's party stood before her respectfully with their heads uncovered and broke the news as gently as possible. Beal read the death warrant while she listened patiently, then, crossing herself, she said that although she was sorry it came from Elizabeth, she had been expecting it for some time and was prepared to die: 'For many years, I have lived in continual affliction, unable to do good to myself or to those who are dear to me and as I shall depart innocent of the crime which has been laid to my charge, I cannot see why I should shrink from the prospect of immortality.'

175

She then solemnly swore on the New Testament that she had neither devised, plotted or consented to the death of the Queen of England. The Earl of Kent, with more zeal than wisdom, objected to the validity of this oath because it was made on a Catholic version of the Bible, but Mary replied that since it was the version whose truth she believed in, her oath should be all the more valid. She was advised to allow the Dean of Peterborough, whom they had brought with them, to console her. She declined, declaring that she would die in the faith in which she had lived, and begged them to allow her to see her Catholic confessor, who had been barred from visiting her for some time, but they forbade it.

Before dying, Mary was anxious to be brought up to date with the events that had led up to her sentence. Had no foreign princes intervened on her behalf? Were her secretaries still alive? Was it intended to punish them as well as her? Did they bring no letters from Elizabeth or others? And above all, was her son, the King of Scotland, well, and had he shown any interest in the fate of a mother who had always loved and never wronged him?

Once each of these points had been discussed, she asked when her execution was to take place. Shrewsbury replied that it was fixed for 8 a.m. the next morning. She seemed shocked and agitated for a few minutes, saying that it was sooner than she had expected, and she had yet to make her will because she had been hoping for the return of the papers and letters that had been taken from her. She soon regained her composure, however, informed the commissioners that she wished to be left alone to make her preparations and dismissed them for the night.

During this scene, her devoted attendants had been overcome by astonishment, indignation and grief. As soon as the earls and their retinue left, they gave full vent to their feelings, only Mary remaining calm. Bourgoine, her physician, railed against the speed with which she was to be dispatched – even the lowest criminal was allowed more than a few hours' notice. Mary told him that she must resign herself to her fate and learn to accept it as the will of God. She then asked them all to kneel with her, and they prayed together for some time.

Afterwards, while supper was being prepared, she divided all the money she had with her into separate purses, labelling each one with the name of the intended recipient. Although she sat down with them at the supper table, she ate and spoke little but smiled placidly every now and then. Her unworldly calmness only made her servants more distressed, as they knew that this was the last meal they would ever share.

As soon as the melancholy supper was over, Mary asked for a cup of wine, and drank a toast to each of her attendants in turn. She asked them to return the compliment, and as each kneeled tearfully and drank to her, they asked her to pardon all the faults they had ever committed. In the true spirit of Christian humility she not only willingly forgave them but asked in turn for their pardon if she had ever forgotten her duty towards them. She implored them to remain faithful to their religion and to live in peace and charity with each other and with all others.

The inventory of her wardrobe and furniture was then brought to her, and she wrote in the margin opposite each article the name of the person she wished to receive it. She did the same with her rings, jewels and her most valuable trinkets, and there was not one of her friends or servants, either present or absent, to whom she forgot to leave a memento.

Having sent a message to her confessor elsewhere in the castle, asking him to pray for her through the night and instruct her which passages from scripture he felt she should study at this point, she then sat down at her desk to arrange her papers, finish her will and write several letters. Her will covered two large sheets of paper. She named as her four executors her cousin, the Duke of Guise, her ambassador in France, the Archbishop of Glasgow, Lesley, Bishop of Ross, and her chancellor, Monsieur de Ruysseau.

She next wrote a letter to her brother-in-law, the King of France, apologizing for being unable to write at greater length because she had only an hour or two to live and had not been informed until just after dinner that she was to be executed next morning, ending by asking him to protect and reward her faithful followers.

Around 2 a.m. she sealed up her papers and said she would now think no more of the affairs of this world but would spend the rest of her time in prayer and examining her own conscience. She went to bed for some hours but did not sleep, her lips moving in continual silent prayer.

On the morning of Wednesday 8 February, Mary rose at daybreak, and her servants, who had stayed awake weeping all night, immediately gathered round her. She told them that she had made her will and asked them to ensure that her executors received it. She said they were not to separate until they had carried her body to France, and she gave her physician a sum of money to meet the expenses of the journey. She expressed the wish to be buried either in the Church of St Denis in Paris, beside her first husband, Francis, or at Rheims, in the same tomb as her mother. Apart from her friends and servants, she asked that a number of poor people and children from various hospitals be invited to attend her funeral, clothed in mourning at her expense, each carrying in their hand a lighted taper, according to the Catholic custom.

She and her servants were praying when there was a knock at the door. A messenger from the commissioners announced that all was ready. She asked for a little longer to finish her prayers, and as soon as she was ready, the sheriff, carrying the white wand of office, entered to take her to the place of execution. Her servants crowded round her, demanding to be allowed to accompany her to the scaffold, but Elizabeth had forbidden this, so they were told that Mary must proceed alone. They protested in vain, and as soon as the door closed behind Mary, the grief-stricken shrieks of the women and the scarcely less audible wailings of the men could be heard all over the castle.

At the foot of the staircase leading down to the hall below, Mary was met by the Earls of Kent and Shrewsbury and was allowed to bid farewell to Sir Andrew Melville, the master of her household. Melville knelt before her with tears in his eyes, kissed her hand and declared that it was the saddest hour of his life. Mary assured him that the same wasn't true for her: 'I now feel, my good Melville, that all this world is vanity. When you speak of me hereafter, mention that I died firm in my faith, willing to forgive my enemies, conscious

179

that I had never disgraced Scotland, my native country, and rejoicing in the thought that I had always been true to France, the land of my happiest years. Tell my son' – at this point her feelings overcame her and tears filled her eyes – 'tell my son that I thought of him in my last moments, and that I have never yielded, either by word or deed, to aught that might lead to his prejudice; desire him to preserve the memory of his unfortunate parent, and may he be a thousand times more happy and more prosperous than she has been.'

Mary turned to the commissioners and told them that her three last requests were that her secretary, Curl, whom she blamed less for his treachery than Nawe, should not be punished, that her servants should be permitted to travel to France, and that some of them should be allowed to witness her death. The earls answered that they believed the first two requests would be granted but not the last, claiming that her attendants' grief would only add to her suffering. But Mary was determined that some of her own people would witness her last moments: 'I will not submit to the indignity of permitting my body to fall into the hands of strangers. You are the servants of a maiden Queen, and she herself, were she here, would yield to the dictates of humanity, and permit some of those who have been so long faithful to me to assist me at my death. Remember, too, that I am cousin to your mistress, and the descendant of Henry VII; I am the Dowager of France, and the anointed Queen of Scotland.' Shamed into complying, the earls allowed her to nominate four male and two female attendants to remain beside her for the short time she had left.

The execution was to take place in the same hall where the

trial had been held, which now contained an expectant crowd of about two hundred people, including Sir Amias Paulet with a body of guards, the other commissioners and some gentlemen of the neighbourhood. At one end, behind a railing, stood the scaffold, about two feet high and covered with black cloth, with a chair set out ready for the Queen of Scots. On one side of the block stood two executioners, and on the other the Earls of Kent and Shrewsbury, with Beal and the sheriff immediately behind them.

Mary entered, leaning on the arm of her physician, while Sir Andrew Melville carried the train of her robe. She looked as if she were attending a reception at court, dressed in a gown of black silk bordered with crimson velvet, over which was a satin mantle. A long veil of white crepe stiffened with wire and edged with rich lace hung down almost to the ground, round her neck she wore an ivory crucifix, and a set of rosary beads was fastened to her girdle.

The symmetry of her fine figure had long been destroyed by her sedentary lifestyle, and years of stress had left many a trace on her beautiful features, but her queenly dignity was still apparent as with a steady step she passed through the hall and ascended the scaffold.

She listened unmoved while Beal read out the death warrant. Once Beal had finished, the Dean of Peterborough appeared at the foot of the scaffold and with more zeal than sensitivity addressed Mary on the subject of her religion. She mildly told him she had been born a Catholic and was resolved to die one, and asked him not to annoy her any longer with useless arguments. When it became obvious he was determined to continue, she turned away from him, fell on her

181

knees and prayed aloud, reciting passages from the psalms. She prayed for her own soul, and that God would send his holy spirit to comfort her in the agony of death. She prayed for all good monarchs, for the Queen of England, for her son, the King of Scotland, for her friends, and for all her enemies. Her earnest delivery and occasional self-assured gestures deeply affected all around her. She clasped a small crucifix in her hands and raised them to heaven, and at intervals a convulsive sob choked her voice.

As soon as her prayers were finished, she prepared to lay her head on the block. As they helped her remove her veil and head-dress, her two female attendants were trembling so violently that they were hardly able to stand. Mary gently reproved them: 'Be not thus overcome. I am happy to leave the world, and you also ought to be happy to see me die so willingly.'

As she bared her neck, she took from around it a gold cross which she wanted to give to Jane Kennedy, but with brutal coarseness the executioner objected, claiming it as one of the perks of his job. 'My good friend,' said Mary, 'she will pay you much more than its value,' but he just snatched it roughly from her hand. She turned away and pronounced a parting blessing on her servants, kissed each of them and bade them farewell.

Ready now, she asked Jane Kennedy to bind her eyes with a rich handkerchief bordered with gold that she had brought with her for the purpose. Laying her head on the block, her last words were: 'O Lord, in Thee I have hoped, and into Thy hands I commit my spirit.'

Either from nerves, lack of skill or because the axe was

blunt, the executioner had to take three blows to separate Mary's head from her body. When his assistant lifted the severed head by the hair and called out 'God save Elizabeth, Queen of England!', the Earl of Kent added: 'Thus perish all her enemies.' Overpowered by the solemnity and horror of the scene, no one responded 'Amen!'

Her servants gathered round Mary's remains, but the body was immediately removed to an adjoining apartment where a piece of old green baize from a billiard table was unceremoniously thrown over it. After a while, perhaps to salve her conscience, Elizabeth ordered it to be embalmed and buried with royal pomp in Peterborough Cathedral.

The Archbishop of Bruges was appointed to preach the sermon at Mary's memorial service in the church of Notre Dame in Paris: 'Many of us have seen in this very place the Queen whom we now deplore, on her bridal morning, and in her royal robes, so resplendent with jewels, that they shone like the light of day, or like her own beauty, which was more resplendent stil. . . . It seemed as if the overwhelming brilliancy of our age was destined to surpass the richest pomp of every preceding age, even the times when Greece and Rome were in all their splendour. A brief space has passed away like a cloud, and we have seen her a captive whom we saw in triumph – a prisoner, who set the prisoners free – poor, who gave away so liberally – disdained, who was the fountain of honour. We have seen her, who was a twofold queen, in the hands of a common executioner, and that fair form, which graced the nuptial couch of the greatest monarch in Christendom, dishonoured on a scaffold. We have seen that loveliness, which was one of the wonders of the world, broken

down by long captivity, and at length effaced by an igno-
minious death. If this fatal reverse teaches the uncertainty
and vanity of all human things, the patience and incompara-
ble fortitude of the Queen we have lost, also teach a more
profitable lesson, and afford a salutary consolation. . . . Others leave to their successors the care of building monuments,
to preserve their name from oblivion; but the life and death
of this lady are her monument. Marble, and brass, and iron
decay, or are devoured by rust; but in no age, however long
the world may endure, will the memory of Mary Stuart,
Queen of Scots, and Dowager of France, cease to he cherished with affection and admiration.'

Twenty-five years later, James VI, wishing to do belated
justice to the memory of his mother, ordered her remains to
be removed from Peterborough to Henry VII's Chapel in
Westminster Abbey, where a splendid monument was
erected. If the inscription on it is to be believed, James must
have blushed with shame and indignation whenever he
thought of his mother's fate.

Mary Stuart, Queen of Scots, was only forty-four when
she died. She was one of the most accomplished and talented
women of the age, as even her enemies had to admit. But
accomplishments do not always lead to happiness, and talents
do not always ensure success. In France she might perhaps
have avoided the evils that overtook her, but in Scotland the
refined manners of a foreign court were hardly suited to cop-
ing with the turbulent spirit, the fanatical enthusiasm and the
semi-barbarous prejudices of the times.

All the most important events of her life happened between the ages of sixteen and twenty-five, when she sought

asylum in England, and her failings could be attributed to youth and lack of experience. A passionate person with an unsuspicious, generous, forgiving nature, time would probably have taught her to temper her idealism with a more realistic view of human nature. She formed attachments too rashly and was too trusting, often finding – when it was too late – that she had been deceived by the strong, ambitious characters who peopled her court. As a result she came to mistrust her own judgment and relied on the guidance of others. This contributed to her downfall.

However, the situation in which she found herself – the heavy responsibilities thrust upon her, the restlessness of the times in which she lived, the unreliable and scheming courtiers who surrounded her, her subjects' deep-rooted prejudices against her Catholicism, the restless jealousy and not entirely unwarranted suspicion of the queen who reigned over the neighbouring and more powerful country of England, her unfortunate marriage to Darnley – would have challenged a far more experienced person. Her main problem was that she was too easily influenced. Had Mary been vain, headstrong, opinionated and bigoted, she would never have yielded so easily to public opinion, she would not have submitted to Knox's insults to her person and her faith, she would never have been dominated by Moray and she would have been less willing to forgive those who opposed her.

But if all her faults can be traced to an excess of pleasant qualities, why did her life end so miserably? Bad luck and lack of experience alone cannot account for her fate. True, her reign was marked by a succession of setbacks, but –

sometimes by the skin of her teeth – she managed to survive them all through her own strength of character. It took the murder of Darnley, Bothwell's subsequent treason and violence, the treachery of Morton, the craftiness of Moray, the disastrous defeat at Langside and the fatal error of judgment which led her to throw herself on the mercy of Elizabeth, the very person who had encouraged her rebellious lords to plot against her, to finally overcome her. The rest of her life would be spent trying to escape from the consequences of that final momentary lapse.

Although Mary came from a very privileged background, almost all her advantages were counterbalanced by disadvantages that accompanied them. She became a queen very soon after she was born, but she was also an orphan. From early childhood she was destined to be the wife of the future monarch of France, but as a result she was taken away from her native country and her mother's arms. Her uncles in the House of Guise may have constantly exerted their power and talents on her behalf, but this meant that she was afflicted by the hatred and jealousy with which they were regarded by many, both at home and abroad. Her residence and education at the court of Henry II of France refined her manners and cultivated her mind, but it also excited suspicion and fear among the people of Scotland. Her beauty may have been legendary, but it won her as much envy as praise. She was deeply loved by her first husband, Francis, but this made her grief at his death all the worse. She returned to her own kingdom as the dowager queen of France, but her power and claim to the throne worried the English and did not prevent her heretical subjects flouting her authority. She married

Darnley in the hope of improving her prospects and finding happiness, but he blighted both. His death may have freed her from his wayward irresponsibility, but what she escaped to was a thousand times worse. She loved Moray, her brother, and loaded him with favours, but he repaid her by stealing her throne and chasing her from the country. She escaped into England but found reproaches instead of assistance, a prison instead of asylum, a mortal enemy instead of a sister, and an axe and a scaffold instead of sympathy and protection.

Had Mary been a prosperous and successful queen, her virtues would be beyond dispute. Human nature, however, is prone to look for guilt as a cause of misery, especially when the mighty are fallen, and suspicions abound to this day that Mary was implicated in the plot to kill Darnley, was too easily won over by Bothwell, and was not unhappy to be championed as a Catholic challenger to Elizabeth's throne. But if one weighs the temptations Mary was exposed to – her youth, her power, the prejudices of her education and the designing ministers who surrounded her – against her conduct towards the Reformers, towards her enemies, towards her friends, indeed towards all her subjects, it is unlikely that she had it in her nature to be underhand.

In the good times, the vivacity and sweetness of her manners, her openness, her candour, her generosity, her polished wit, her extensive knowledge, her cultivated taste, her easy affability, her powers of conversation, her natural dignity and grace were all conspicuous – although too little appreciated by the less refined characters who populated the Scottish court during this period. But her character was no less admirable in times of trouble – on the contrary, they gave her the opportunity to display a courage and nobility that even she might not have known she possessed if she had never experienced adversity.

Her piety and her constancy became even more apparent in prison than on the throne. In victory, it is easy for a conquering monarch to court popularity, but it is far more difficult to overcome the natural weaknesses of one's own nature and, in the midst of suffering, triumph over one's enemies. Mary managed to do this, and she was to be envied a thousand times more when kneeling at her solitary devotions in Fotheringay Castle than Elizabeth, surrounded with all the heartless splendour of Hampton Court.

As Mary laid her head on the block, the serene way she confronted death put all her enemies to shame. Mary was not destined to wear the crown of England, but she gained instead the crown of a martyr.